Traveling with Martin Luther

D1598354

A Biographical Guidebook

Traveling with Martin Luther

Cornelia Dömer

CONCORDIA PUBLISHING HOUSE · SAINT LOUIS

The information in this guidebook has been carefully researched. However, please keep in mind that some information is susceptible to change. The publishing house is not responsible for implications from the use of this guidebook or for any information listed in any of the Web sites.

We value your opinion. If you have any suggestions that would improve this guidebook, please let us know.

English translation copyright © 2010 Concordia Publishing House
3558 S. Jefferson Avenue, St. Louis, MO 63118-3968
1-800-325-3040 • www.cph.org

Translated by Nicholas D. Proksch and Christian C. Tiews

German edition, Dr. Cornelia Dömer, *Mit Martin Luther unterwegs*
© copyright 2008 by SCM Hänssler, D-71088 Holzgerlingen, Germany

Cover images: istockphoto.com

Maps: Goldjunge Grafik & Design, Stuttgart; www.gold-junge.com

Manufactured in China

1 2 3 4 5 6 7 8 9 10   19 18 17 16 15 14 13 12 11 10

Contents

Introduction

God anchored human life in the soil from which He drew us. Our lives unfold in specific places, in the context of physical surroundings as well as in a community of human beings. Knowing where people come from enriches our understanding of them. Such knowledge includes not only the intellectual and spiritual contexts in which they grew up but also their geographic origin. This is true of living people we know and also of historical figures who interest us.

This volume is both for tourists and for those who do not leave their own homes far from Martin Luther's German homeland. It enables readers who will never see Luther's native turf to imagine more precisely how his life unfolded in the surroundings in which God called him to serve His Church. It also provides a most helpful preparation for those who want to travel to the "Lutherlands" and see the sites themselves. It is the tourist's *vademecum*, to be thumbed through while one walks through the streets and reviewed evenings after or before following in the reformer's footsteps.

The author leads us through landmarks of Luther's life—from the ancestral home in Möhra to his birthplace, Eisleben, and on to Mansfeld, where he grew up. Dömer accompanies us to the cities where Luther received his education, to the lonely spot where he decided to become a monk, and especially to Wittenberg, where small-town life and the activities of a young university made their imprint on him even as he made his on them. With glimpses of other towns that played a longer or shorter role in his story, this volume leads readers through the reformer's career. Dömer's effective recounting of the events of Luther's biography sets the framework for viewing the visuals that make this book unique. Attractive photographs and clearly presented maps stimulate the imagination and afford a useful orientation for learning more about the reformer's life and for truly understanding this particular human being by gaining a better idea of the particular surroundings in which he lived. The tools are here for guiding the reader's imagination into Luther's world.

Such a volume cannot include every place Luther visited. Despite being declared an outlaw by the German emperor, he traveled, for instance, to Smalcald and to Marburg. In the former city, in 1537, Luther made clear that the heart of his message was that "Jesus Christ, our God and Lord, 'was handed over to death for our trespasses and was raised for our justification' . . . he alone is 'the Lamb of God who takes away the sin of the world'" (Smalcald Articles II II 1–2). "On this article," Luther added, "stands all that we teach and practice" (Smalcald Articles II II 5). In 1529 he traveled to Marburg, where visitors can still see the table at which he sat with his supporter-turned-antagonist Ulrich Zwingli. They disagreed over the presence of Christ in the Lord's Supper. Luther insisted that God conveys the Gospel to sinners through the bread and wine that, in a mysterious manner, truly deliver Christ's body and blood; through the Sacrament, God continues to deliver "for you" forgiveness of sins, life, and salvation. Luther found great comfort in the fact that the Holy Spirit exercises the power of salvation through His Word in oral, written, and also sacramental forms.

Many of Luther's own students regarded him as superhuman, and admirers across the centuries have difficulty focusing on the reality of this ordinary man who possessed great gifts. A picture of the reformer that does not reflect the reality of his environmental and geographic situation lessens the benefits gained from studying his life and thought. This volume enhances the reader's ability to grasp the life of this servant of God's Word. It therefore enables us to grasp the significance of Luther's message more fully.

Robert Kolb
Missions Professor Emeritus of Systematic Theology
Concordia Seminary
St. Louis, Missouri
October 2009

Preface

Martin Luther changed the world. At the zenith of the change from the Middle Ages to the modern era stand Luther's Ninety-five Theses from the year 1517 and their defense in 1521 before the imperial meeting at Worms. What was an incomparable demand for the representatives of power in church and state was, for others, an act of liberation from the guardianship of precisely these powers toward radical trust only in the mercy of God, which is valid for all people equally. Thus a consciousness developed of one's own, immediate responsibility before God and human beings, as even today, in the preamble of the constitution of Germany, it is exalted as the highest moral maxim.

The breakthrough to a new thought, to a new understanding of generally obligatory, basic values, and to a new culture of life in politics, religion, and society had been accompanied by passionate conflicts and battles by hook or by crook. In the heart of Europe, the names of places still shine that served as the theater of history about five hundred years ago: for example, the Luther cities Eisenach and Wittenberg, Worms and Augsburg, the Augustinian Cloister in Erfurt, and the Wartburg in Eisenach, to name only a few.

It is, in my opinion, a great idea to give people a biographical tour guide, in order to be able once again to seek out these theaters of history at the side of Martin Luther; to reread what, when, and where it happened; and, above all, to let Luther himself be "located" through corresponding quotations.

To the places and events belong the people who accompanied Luther along his path in a special way, whether as glowing fans or bitter opponents, as students or learned disputants, as artists or politicians, as friends or family members—with Katharina von Bora, the "Lutheress," at the front. These individuals, too, are discussed in great variety in this biographical tour guide, and they become recognizable not only in their significance for Luther personally but also for the course of the Reformation and historical processes in general.

A multitude of historical and modern texts, pictures, and points of information, of addresses and references to literature, make this tour guide—which is likely the only one of its kind—an interesting, informative, and useful companion for all who would like to know something of the background, and to have it come to the fore.

Hänssler Verlag and the author, Cornelia Dömer, are to be thanked for their timely work in making this tour guide available before the great date 2017 (the 500th anniversary of Luther's posting of the Ninety-five Theses in Wittenberg). Many people with very different interests will make the journey from all parts of the world in order to walk in the footsteps of Luther and the Reformation in this or that region of Germany. Among them will be many people from the worldwide group of about seventy million who, as Lutherans, bear this German family name in the emblems of their churches. But it is not only about them. May this biographical tour guide help them as well as all others to encounter the *genius loci* concretely and intelligently at the places of the events, and to notice a bit of the great breadth of God's love and mercy, which moved, drove, and comforted Luther.

In all of this, the point is not to venerate Martin Luther as a hero. Beside the ingenious accomplishments and testimonies of faith, his weaknesses are also recorded critically—and even, in part, his fatal errors, such as in his utterances against the Jews. The multiform composition and the breadth of content of this biographical tour guide reflect the extensive experiences of Cornelia Dömer, which she was able to gather internationally and ecumenically through many years as leader of the Luther Center in Wittenberg. Traveling with Luther is fun!

Dr. Christian Krause

Territorial Bishop, retired

President of the Lutheran World Federation, 1997–2003

Wolfenbüttel, July 2008

Foreword

Meeting Martin Luther

Ranking in third place in *Life* magazine's list of the most important persons of the previous millennium, Martin Luther triggered monumental changes with his ideas and writings.

Luther did not reach his real goal, which was to reform the entire Roman Catholic Church. Yet his unique insight—namely, that man receives the grace of God by faith alone—spread across all of Europe and, shortly thereafter, even around the globe.

Luther's translation of the Bible into German from its original languages of Hebrew and Greek had a decisive impact on German-speaking lands, which until that point had been splintered into a number of different dialects.

I am greatly indebted to the well-known Luther scholar Professor Martin Brecht. Many of the facts and much of the background information contained in this book are directly or indirectly from him, and I wish to thank him for his approval.

Cornelia Dömer

Göppingen, Germany

September 2008

Discover the traces of a man who changed the world. Down through the centuries, he has left his tracks. Eisleben built this monument to Martin Luther more than one hundred years ago.

The great reformer was born in this house.

CHAPTER ONE
The Roots

The Region of Mansfeld—Luther's Childhood

Not much is known about Luther's childhood. He was born on November 10, 1483, in Eisleben as the second[1] son of a miner named Hans Luder (originally from Möhra in Thuringia) and his wife, Margarete.

Only one day after his birth, Luther was baptized in the Church of Saints Peter and Paul (*St.-Petri-Pauli-Kirche*) in Eisleben. The infant was named after the saint of that particular day: Martin.

Sights in Möhra

Luther Monument
(*Lutherdenkmal*)

The Luther Monument in Möhra was commissioned in 1846 to be erected by sculptor Ferdinand Müller. It was dedicated in 1861.

Leaving many relatives behind, in 1484 Luther's father, Hans, moved his small family to Mansfeld. Even today, "Luther" is one of the most common last names in this region.

Hans Luder was able to climb the social ladder in Mansfeld. Starting out as a miner, he later owned a copper mine and eventually even became a city councilor (*Ratsherr*). Martin's upbringing was somber and marked by thriftiness and strictness.

At the age of only four and a half, Martin was enrolled at the local "trivium school" (*Trivialschule*), similar to our modern elementary schools. Martin's memories of this city school,

The massive castle of the counts of Mansfeld towers over a steep valley.

however, were not especially pleasant, since beatings with a rod and other punishments were standard fare. Martin attended this school until 1497.

Commenting on his family background and ancestors, Martin Luther wrote:

> I am the son of a peasant. My great-grandfather, grandfather, and father were truly peasants. But my father insisted I should become a director, a mayor [*Schultheiss*], or whatever else they have in the village—a chief servant, rising above the others. Later, my father moved to Mansfeld and became a miner there. That is where I am from.[2]

1 Home of Luther's parents (*Luthers Elternhaus*)

2 Luther's home church, Church of St. George (*St. Georg*)

3 Luther Monument (Luther Fountain) (*Lutherbrunnen*)

4 Luther's school (*Luthers Schule*)

5 Mansfeld Castle (*Schloss Mansfeld*)

i Tourist Information

Sights in Mansfeld

(For Eisleben, see chapter 11)

Home of Luther's Parents (*Luthers Elternhaus*)

In 1483/84, Luther's father moved from Eisleben to Mansfeld, where they rented a house. The original address was Am Stufenberg 2. Today, the address of that building is Spangenbergstrasse 2.

Luther's Home Church, the Church of St. George (*St. Georg*)

This church was built in the Late Gothic style between 1497 and 1518. We can assume that young Luther served as an acolyte in the earlier sanctuary, which had been constructed in the Romanesque period and of which some sections are still preserved. In addition to a painting of the resurrection by Lucas Cranach the Elder, this church also boasts the only full-length portrait of Luther painted in Cranach's workshop.[3]

Luther Monument (*Lutherdenkmal*)

The Luther Fountain in Luther Square was constructed in 1913 by Paul Juckoff. It depicts Luther as a thirteen-year-old boy with a staff.

Luther's Elementary School (*Luthers Schule*)

In 1488, Luther attended the City School of Mansfeld (*Mansfelder Stadtschule*) for the first time. It is here that he learned to read, write, and do arithmetic. This is also where he acquired basic Latin skills.

Mansfeld Castle (*Schloss Mansfeld*)

Documented for the first time in 1229, this castle was the ancestral seat of the counts of Mansfeld. Today, it is home to the local YMCA (CVJM).

Magdeburg and Eisenach—School Years

At the age of fourteen, Luther transferred to the school of the Brothers of the Common Life in Magdeburg. At fifteen, he switched to the Latin School of St. George in Eisenach, preparing for university. While it is unknown why Luther switched schools, it was not unusual in that era, especially when pupils came from a village that did not offer further educational opportunities, as was the case in Mansfeld.

Luther was accompanied to Magdeburg by his friend Hans Reinecke, and he lived in the home of Dr. Paul Mosshauer, a representative of the archbishop at clerical proceedings. Mosshauer, too, was from Mansfeld and had relatives there who had become masters in the trade of mining. Most likely, it was

The Old Town section of Magdeburg.

Mosshauer's recommendation that prompted Luther to attend school in Magdeburg. The reason Luther then transferred to Eisenach was probably because he had relatives there.

Sights in Magdeburg

Church of St. John, with Luther Monument (*Johanneskirche mit Lutherdenkmal*)

The foundation of this church was laid between 936 and 941. It was first documented in 941, when it was mentioned as a parish church, which had been given to the Monastery of St. Maurice (Moritz) by King Otto I.

Luther preached here in 1524 on the topic of true and false justice. The reformer's sermon made such a huge impression on his listeners that the city became Lutheran soon thereafter.

In fact, Emil Hundrieser designed a Luther statue in 1886 in memory of this sermon. The statue's original pedestal had been replaced by a concrete foundation in 1966. On May 29, 1995, the original pedestal was put in place once again, along with the inscription: "God's Word with us eternally."

The Walloons' Church (*Wallonerkirche*)

This church was founded in 1285 by monks of the Augustinian Monastery. Jubilee indulgences were celebrated in 1396, and because Magdeburg was appointed as the only place to offer such pardons within a sixty-kilometer (approximately forty-mile) radius, it drew many pilgrims.

Luther visited this church and its Augustinian monks in 1516, spending the night in one of the monastery's dormitory rooms. In 1524, he came for another visit and preached there. That same year, the abbot dissolved the monastery and handed over all its facilities to the city of Magdeburg. From then on, the church was used only for secular purposes. After the Thirty Years' War, it was no longer repaired, and it was no longer used after 1639.

In 1690, by order of Elector Frederick William, the church was handed over to Lutheran Walloon refugees, and since that time, it has been known as the Walloons' Church.

Cathedral (*Dom*)

As early as 955—that is, even before being crowned emperor—Otto I began building a cathedral in Magdeburg in the Ottonian-Romanesque style. It was the predecessor of the modern-day cathedral and beautifully adorned. In 1207, fire destroyed the cathedral and most of the city of Magdeburg.

Years later, a new cathedral was constructed next to the old one by using the original rocks and pillars. The Reformation had an impact on the cathedral: after being shuttered for twenty years, it was reopened in 1567 and became Lutheran—celebrating its first Lutheran church service on the First Sunday in Advent of that year.

1 Church of St. John, with Luther Monument (*Johanniskirche*)

2 Walloons' Church (*Wallonerkirche*)

3 Cathedral of Saints Maurice and Catherine (*Dom St. Mauritius und St. Katharina*)

i Tourist Information

Photographed in 2008 with scaffolding, the Wartburg Castle was where Luther found refuge and the time to translate the New Testament.

CHAPTER TWO

Eisenach
and Wartburg Castle

Luther spent happy years in Eisenach, which is why he was soon able to call that town, "Eisenach, his dear city."

Eisenach in Luther's Day

Around 1500, Eisenach's population had probably dropped to slightly more than 4,000, since the former capital no longer contained the prince's residence. However, there were still more clergy in Eisenach during that period than would have been customary for an average city. Eisenach had three parish churches: the Church of St. Nicholas, associated with a monastery; the Church of St. George, which had sixteen altars and curates; and, finally, the Church of St. Mary (*Marienstift*), which had twenty altars and curates. On top of that, the Dominicans, Franciscans, and Carthusians all had monasteries in town. As such, religious life in Eisenach was rich and multifaceted.

At times, young Luther earned his sustenance by singing in front of homes and being rewarded with bread. This was customary for pupils in that era, and it taught them to be frugal.

Later, Heinrich Schalbe—mayor from 1495 to 1499—took Luther in. Schalbe's son was practically the same age as Luther and attended the same school, St. George, which was named after the neighboring church. It was here that Luther participated in the cult of St. Anne, which was extremely popular at that time. Luther's beloved teacher, Johannes Braun, and many of his fellow students took part in this as well. Luther stayed in contact with his former teacher even after entering the monastery. During this period, Luther's deep sense of Roman Catholic piety was formed.

St. Anne

According to the apocryphal Gospels (that is, the false Gospels written between the second and sixth centuries AD), Anne and Joachim were the parents of Mary and, as such, the grandparents of Jesus. Their legendary life story bears a remarkable resemblance to that of Hannah and her son Samuel in the Old Testament (1 Samuel 1–2), with Anne giving birth to Mary after twenty years of barren marriage.

From the sixth century on, Anne was venerated as the mother of Mary. In Europe, the cult of Anne peaked in the Late Middle Ages, when in 1481 Pope Sixtus IV included a day of commemoration for Anne in the calendar of the Roman Catholic Church. In 1584, Pope Gregory XIII designated July 26 as her festival day. Supposedly from 1500 on, relics of St. Anne were kept in Düren, Vienna, and elsewhere.

St. Anne is the patron saint for thunderstorms. Around St. Anne's Day in late July, the "dog days of summer" begin and last until early August. That time of year is determined by the rise of Sirius, the "Dog Star," in the constellation of Canis Major ("Great Dog"). Heat waves, which trigger thunderstorms, are common during that time of year.[4]

Luther House in Eisenach. It is said that Luther lived here as a pupil.

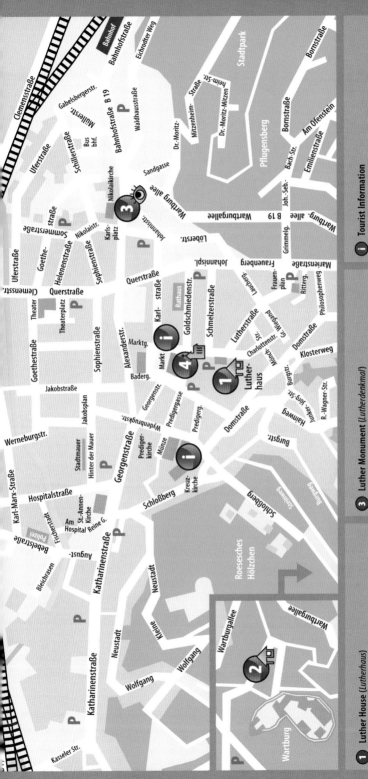

1 Luther House (*Lutherhaus*)
2 Wartburg
3 Luther Monument (*Lutherdenkmal*)
4 Church of St. George (*Georgenkirche*)
i Tourist Information

Sights in Eisenach

Luther House (*Lutherhaus*)

One of the oldest half-timbered structures in Eisenach, Luther House belonged to the Cotta family for many years. According to an old tradition, Martin Luther lived in this house while attending school in Eisenach (1498–1501).

Beginning in 1898, the building was the home of the *Lutherkeller*, a restaurant specializing in traditional German cuisine. Both of Luther's rooms have been open to the public from that period on. Damaged in World War II, the building was repaired and the state church of Thuringia established a Luther memorial there in 1956.

Wartburg Castle

First documented in 1080, the Wartburg belonged to the noble family of the Ludowingians. The historically renowned palace was added between 1156 and 1162, after which the Wartburg changed hands.

The Wartburg is a classical example of a "linear castle." Originally composed of four sections—of which only the front and main castle remain today—the Wartburg was besieged many times yet never conquered. It was made famous by two of its residents—Luther and Elisabeth of Thuringia[5]—and is one of Germany's national monuments.

Luther Monument (*Lutherdenkmal*)

Constructed in 1895 by Adolf Donndorf, it is located in Eisenach's Karlsplatz.

Church of St. George (*Georgenkirche*)

The Church of St. George is the main church in Eisenach's Old Town. This is the church in which Martin Luther preached immediately after the beginning of the Reformation, which he triggered. It thus became one of the oldest Lutheran churches in the world.

Elisabeth of Thuringia (Elisabeth of Hungary)

Elisabeth was born in 1207 in Hungary and died November 17, 1231, in Marburg.

The daughter of King Andrew II of Hungary and Gertrude of Carinthia-Andechs-Merania, Elisabeth was born in the year the famous "Wartburg contest"—a competition among troubadours—took place at the Wartburg near Eisenach. According to poems and legends, the sorcerer Klingsor of Hungary visited the castle and prophesied that the king would have a daughter, namely Elisabeth.

Ludwig IV, son of the landgrave of Thuringia, married Elisabeth in 1221 when she was only fourteen years old.

Ludwig and Elisabeth had a happy marriage and were soon blessed with three children, the youngest of whom was Gertrude. In 1225, the first Franciscans came to Eisenach. They idealized poverty, making a huge impression on Elisabeth and prompting her to care for and visit the poor. Although her husband supported her in this endeavor, her family viewed her actions with great suspicion. But detailed legends describe how Elisabeth would not be deterred by the slander and criticism of those close to her.

Various miracles are accredited to St. Elisabeth. For example, she supposedly once let a leprous man rest in her marital bed, but when the sheets were pulled back, not the leprous man but the crucified Christ Himself became visible. In 1226, there was a great famine. Elisabeth had all available grain distributed to the people and even provided money from the treasury for them. When she was vehemently accosted with criticism, it is said that the floor of the great hall was suddenly covered with grain and that all the storehouses overflowed with grain as well. When Emperor Frederick II came to visit with his entourage, Elisabeth could not find an appropriate gown to wear in her wardrobe. Suddenly, an angel adorned Elisabeth with jewels and such splendor that she looked more majestic than anyone in the room.

While the "miracle of the roses" is not documented in her life story or in the vast collections of legends, the story goes like this: Elisabeth was traveling down into the valley, carrying a carefully covered basket full of bread. Incited by his court to check once again on her wastefulness, Frederick II supposedly came up to her and asked, "What are you carrying?" She uncovered the basket, and he saw nothing but roses.

Recruited for the Fifth Crusade and even receiving a cross from Konrad of Hildesheim, Elisabeth's husband joined the German Order. However, Ludwig fell ill during the voyage off the coast of Brindisi, Italy. After he was brought ashore at Otranto, he died of a disease. Because the empress died at the same place, legend has it that both Ludwig and Empress Jolantha had consumed a deadly poison together. In her tremendous grief, Elisabeth cried out, "It is to me as if the world died with him."

After Ludwig's death, she and her three children were thrown out of Wartburg Castle by her brother-in-law, Heinrich Raspe, who claimed she was wasting public money on alms.

In 1229, Elisabeth moved to Marburg, where her confessor, Konrad of Marburg, lived. This monk belonged to the extremely strict order of the Premonstratensians. Because of his fanatical severity, he was killed in 1233. Elisabeth, however, lived in extreme poverty because she considered it to be virtuous. She went begging from door to door and was determined to relinquish in a final, legally binding manner all the wealth to which the law entitled her. However, to save the wealth for himself, Konrad prevented her from legally relinquishing it. Consequently, Elisabeth used the funds to build a hospital in Marburg in 1229, which she named after St. Francis. She left her children, joined the hospital society run by Konrad, and worked in the hospital as a nurse until she died.

Elisabeth died at the age of twenty-four and was buried at the St. Francis Hospital she had founded.

Elisabeth was canonized only four years after her death. In a vision of Mechthild of Helfta, God Himself is said to have justified her canonization, explaining: "My messengers need to be quick. Elisabeth was and is a messenger whom I sent to women who sit around in castles, are full of selfish pride, arrogant, completely immoral, and wrapped up in vanity. They do not worry about their salvation one little bit. In fact, these women are so wicked that they deserve to go to hell. On the other hand, many other women have followed the example of Elisabeth, as far as their willpower and strength will let them."[6]

Later, the German Order based in Marburg expanded Elisabeth's hospital and built Germany's first Gothic building between 1235 and 1283, a church dedicated to her.[7]

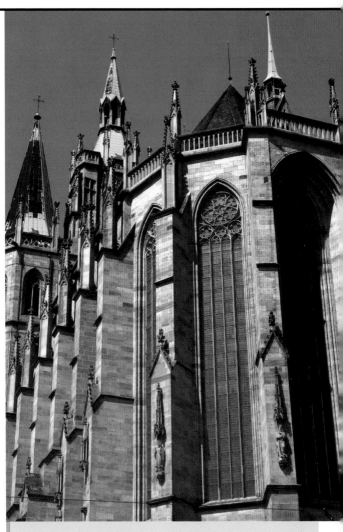
In 1501, Martin Luther enrolled as a student at the University of Erfurt. The impressive Cathedral of St. Mary is the city's landmark.

CHAPTER THREE
Erfurt—Luther, the University Student

The first officially recorded date in Luther's life is the 1501 student attendance roll of the University of Erfurt, which reads: "Martinus ludher ex Mansfeld." This is how we know that Luther began his studies in that year. Before swearing his oath to the dean and university, Luther had to pay his tuition of one-third of a guilder because the registrar's office had considered him to be well-off ("in habendo").

After only three semesters, Luther was able to acquire the first degree of medieval university instructors, the "baccalaureat in artibus," which was a kind of assistantship in the so-called seven liberal arts. These arts included mathematics, music, astronomy, and rhetoric. These skills had to be acquired before one could further his education.

Erfurt in the Late Middle Ages

Erfurt was an economic center at the crossroads of major trade routes within the lowlands of Thuringia, and with a population of about 20,000, it was a large city in Luther's day.

Erfurt's city university was founded in 1392 and demonstrated confidence and economic strength. It was one of the first universities in Germany, was self-regulated, and had an increasingly good reputation.

Politically, however, the city of Erfurt was not in an enviable position. Both the archbishop of Mainz and the elector of Saxony were fighting over it, trying to hinder Erfurt's independence. Furthermore, in a struggle with the archbishopric of Mainz, Erfurt unfortunately sided with the losing party and thus had to declare bankruptcy in 1509. What's more, in that "crazy year," the citizens rebelled against the substantial tax imposed by the four-headed government of the city. In fact, one of its four rulers, Heinrich Keller, was executed the following year.

In other struggles over the city, the peasants sided with Mainz, while the upper class took the side of Saxony, as did Luther, who returned to Erfurt after a temporary stay in Wittenberg.

Luther knew very well how important Erfurt was as the hub of many ecclesiastical institutions, boasting four diocesan churches, twenty-one parish churches, and eleven monastery churches.

The Church of the Barefooted Monks (*Barfüßerkirche*) in Erfurt.

Towering over all of these—geographically and in importance—was the diocese cathedral (*Domstift*), the residence and headquarters of a bishop consecrated by Mainz.

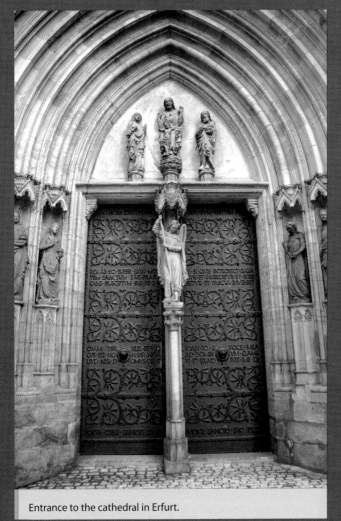

Entrance to the cathedral in Erfurt.

Luther was full of praise for Erfurt:

Erfurt has an excellent location in the fat of the land. That is where a city should be located—even if it were to burn down.[8]

Students tended to live in dormitories called a "Burse." This was true for Luther as well, who during his first two years of college lived in a dormitory called the "Gateway to Heaven" (*Himmelspforte*)—one of the most prestigious dorms in town. The house rules were about as strict as those of a monastery. The residents, so-called "Bursalen," wore clothing according to their academic level. In the Burse itself, students wore a vest, long trousers, and a belt. In public, a coat or robe was worn over this outfit in addition to a head covering. Students were required to study very hard and to speak Latin even outside of class. "Carousing and relationships with the other sex" were prohibited, though the Bursen were allowed to serve alcohol during the hours of operation customary for taverns.

Life was Spartan in the Bursen. The students slept in sleeping halls. Several students shared a workroom. They were awakened at 4 a.m. and went to bed at 8 p.m. Only two meals a day were served. Breakfast was at 10 a.m., and the second meal was at 5 p.m. after lectures. Classes began at 8 a.m. Students attended the church services of the university and of the faculty, and spiritual life continued in the Bursen.

In 1505, Luther became a magister, that is, he was awarded a master's degree in the liberal arts. This academic rank was similar to that of an associate professor today. In his master's examination at the end of the year, Luther ranked second in a class of seventeen. In accordance with his father's wishes, Luther began his law studies on May 19, beginning first with civil law. But on July 17—less than two months later—he joined the Augustinian Order. Luther had experienced a crisis after some of his colleagues and professors had suddenly died of the plague and other diseases. Yet there was also another incident, one that would change his life forever.

Zitadelle Petersberg

Lindenweg
Krämpferstr.
Juri-Gagarin-Ring
Meyfahrtstr.
Weißfraueng.
Trommsdorffstr.
Hospital-platz
Hospital-kirche
Krämpferstr.
Fleischg.
Löweng.
Merfahrtstraße
gasse
Pflückengasse
Mohren-
Kaufmanns-kirche
Krämpfertor
P
Johannesstraße
Schotten-str.
Schotten-kirche
Kaiser-saal
Futterstraße
Meienbergstraße
straße
Lorenz-kirche
Anger
Ursulinen-kirche und -kloster
Johannesstraße
Schottenstr.
Schotteng.
Ägidien-kirche
Wenige markt
Kaufmänner-straße
Seengäßlein
Pilse
Schlösserstraße
Gotthardtstraße
Hirtg.
Schildg.
Dammg.
Horngasse
Krämerbrücke
Rathausbrücke
Kürschnerg.
Pilse
Junkersand
Grafen-gasse
Born gasse
Taschen-gasse
gasse
Augustinerstr.
Nikolai-turm
Tauben-gasse
Comthur-gasse
Kreuzsand
Benedikts-platz
Barfüßerstr.
Studenteng.
Waage gasse
Fisch-markt
Schlösserstraße
Michaelisstraße
Augustinerstraße
Allerheiligenstraße
Pergamenterstraße
gasse
Magdalenen-kapelle
Rumpel-gasse
Predigger-kirche
Meister-Eckehart-Str.
Ziegen-gasse
Georgs-turm
Georgs-
Turnierg.
Pergamentergasse
Kleine Arche
Pauls-turm
straße
Schatten-wandgasse
Marbacher Gasse
Weiße Gasse
Marktstraße
Metteng.
Große Arche
Paul-straße
Nonnen-gasse
Lange Brücke
Kl. Markt
Andreas-kirche
Kl. Andreasstraße
Kettenstr.
Stunzengasse
Polizei
Bechtheimer Straße
Lichtentstr.
Lauentorstraße
Dom-platz
P
Bus
An den Graden
ehemalige Peterskirche
Boni-fazius-turm
Marien-dom
Dom-stufen
Domstraße
Defensions-kaserne
Severi-kirche
Peterstr.
Kommandanten-haus
Wagen-haus
Mainzerhofstr.
Wach-gebäude
Welschstraße
Koenbergkstr.

i Tourist Information

1 Augustinian Monastery (*Augustinerkloster*)

2 Erfurt Cathedral (*Erfurter Dom*)

3 Luther Monument (*Lutherdenkmal*)

4 Old University (*Alte Universität*)

5 The Church of the Barefooted Monks (*Barfüßerkirche*)

6 City Hall (*Rathaus*)

Sights in Erfurt

Augustinian Monastery (*Augustinerkloster*)

The parish church of Saints Phillip and James was constructed in 1131 at the site where the Augustinian Monastery now stands. In 1266, the Augustinians received permission to establish a presence, so they began construction of the monastery in 1277. Funds for construction came from alms and selling indulgences. By 1518, the monastery included a library, the Chapel of St. Catherine, the chapter house,[9] the church steeple, a cloister, a nave, a priory, and woad storehouses. Luther was a member of the monastery from 1505 to 1511 and read his first Mass on May 2, 1507.

Because the order had its own college, the Augustinians became the first theology professors when nearby Erfurt University was founded. Luther attended Erfurt University from 1505 to 1511.

The monastery was secularized during the Reformation, and in 1561 the city of Erfurt built a secondary school in the west wing.

The monastery was renovated after the Iron Curtain fell. Since then, nuns of the Communität Casteller Ring (CCR) have breathed new life into the monastery. Visitors can now be housed in one of fifty rooms that have been renovated with the look and feel of medieval monastery accommodations.

Erfurt Cathedral (*Erfurter Dom*)

Luther was ordained as a priest in this cathedral.

It is believed that a sanctuary was erected at this site in 752. What we know today as the Cathedral of St. Mary was first documented in 1117. Some sections of the original church—built in the Romanesque style—exist even today. However, since the church was deemed too small for the growing number of clerics, it was continually expanded, but in the Gothic style.

The cathedral was damaged in various wars but never destroyed. In 1994 it was designated as the cathedral of the reestablished Diocese of Erfurt.

Luther Monument (*Lutherdenkmal*)

Sculpted by Schaper on the occasion of Luther's 400th birthday (1883), the monument is located on the south side of the Merchants' Church (*Kaufmanns-kirche*). It was dedicated to the citizens of Erfurt on October 31, 1889.

Old University (*Alte Universität*)

The historic University of Erfurt is situated in the so-called Latin Quarter, an area noteworthy for its many structures that are reminiscent of the old university. One such structure is the Collegium Maius—the university's main building—which was destroyed in World War II but has been undergoing reconstruction since 1998. Built between 1512 and 1515, the university's motto is still legible, chiseled in stone above the portal: "Magistra vitae regina rerum possidet sapientia," which means: "Wisdom—the teacher of life and queen of the world—rules here."[10]

The Church of the Barefooted Monks (*Barfüßerkirche*)

Built in 1231, this church originally belonged to a Franciscan monastery. Luther preached here in 1529, four years after the church had become Lutheran.

City Hall (*Rathaus*)

Built in the neo-Gothic style, this structure features murals depicting scenes from Luther's life.

"On their journey, Luther's friend Alexis is struck by lightning" (etching by Gustav König, 1847).

CHAPTER FOUR
Experiences That Changed Luther's Life

Stotternheim

In June 1505, Luther traveled to Mansfeld to visit his parents. Returning to Erfurt on July 2, he was caught in a violent thunderstorm near the village of Stotternheim, located just below the Stollberg range of hills and some six kilometers (four miles) from Erfurt. A bolt of lightning struck the ground near him, probably knocking him down and injuring his leg. Scared to death, he swore, "Help me, St. Anne. I will become a monk." He later said that he was so afraid of being killed that he was forced to make that oath. He "must have thought there was no way to avoid taking this oath,"[11] because—as he always emphasized later[12]—he actually did not want to become a monk.

On July 16, Luther celebrated with his friends one last time and bade them farewell. Luther later wrote the following about his Erfurt years:

> To aspire to a bachelor's degree, yes, even a master's degree, and then to lay down the brown beret, leaving it for others to pursue, and then to become a monk was not the least bit disgraceful. Yet my father became very upset about it. Years later, however, when I had locked horns with the pope, my father and I made up.[13]

The Augustinians

"The Order of the Augustinian Hermits (www.augustiner.de) was established in the middle of the thirteenth century. Interestingly, it was founded not on the initiative of any individual founder— but by order of the pope. Pope Alexander IV decreed that several groups of hermits living in communities in Italy join together and form the Order of Hermits of St. Augustine. The order was named after St. Augustine because the group had accepted the rule of order associated with that church father."[14]

Even in Luther's day, that rule was considered to be very strict. The Augustinian monks rose every morning at 3 a.m., beginning their day with a short prayer service dedicated to St. Mary, which was followed by a long service of prayers and readings called Matins. This service was followed by others: Prime (6 a.m.), Terce (9 a.m.), Sext (noon), None and Vespers (early afternoon), and Compline (before bed). The daily Mass for the monastery was celebrated in the morning. Hymns to St. Mary ("Ave Maria" and "Salve Regina"[15]) were sung after every prayer service. Singing these services was an obligation for every monk.

The Augustinian Monastery in Erfurt. In Luther's day, its strict way of life was hidden behind an idyllic facade.

Apparently for more than a decade, Luther was able to reconcile what he read in his mandatory Bible studies in the monastery with the effusive devotion of the Virgin Mary customary in that environment. He strove with all earnestness to live as a monk, even up to his physical limitations. But even though he accepted the various humiliating tasks assigned to him, he could not keep all the rules despite his diligence. His conscience constantly troubled him because he could not perfectly complete all the canonical hours and his mandatory duties. At the same time, those activities—along with complete weekly confessions—were meant as works of penance to pay for sins.

Luther's superiors at the monastery could not help but notice how intensely Luther studied Scripture and how diligent and intelligent he was. So after only two years, on February 27, 1507, he was ordained as a priest. This new status reconciled Luther with his father, who traveled to Erfurt for the ordination in a carriage pulled by a magnificent team of horses.

Journey to Rome

At that time, the monastery at Erfurt had extremely strict ordinances.[16] They were taken very seriously—as was the order itself—and obeyed by Luther and his fellow monks. Vicar-General[17] Johann von Staupitz had the difficult task of maintaining this strict monastic life. He charged Luther and another monk to travel to Rome in order to address these regulations of the order.

Thus in November 1510, Luther began the longest journey of his life. Traveling southward through Germany, he and his traveling companion stopped at Nuremberg, Ulm, and probably Memmingen. "The journey probably continued along the Rhine valley via Chur and the Septimer Pass to Chiavenna. From there they presumably continued along Lake Como, down to Milan."[18] On the way, the two men had to cross difficult Alpine passes.

In those days, the landscape of Rome had not yet been greatly influenced by the Renaissance. In fact, at that time, only a few churches and buildings had been built in that style. Work on the Basilica of St. Peter had just begun.

But Luther was more interested in his salvation than in Roman architecture. As had already happened twice in Erfurt, he once again wanted to give a general confession in Rome. But to his disgust, Luther's Roman confessors were not interested in hearing him out. Luther was also greatly disappointed that

Masses were being celebrated in a purely mechanical fashion. In fact, within the space of only one hour, he witnessed seven Masses being celebrated in the Basilica of St. Sebastian. Yet none of them met his expectations.

But those were not the only abuses that he saw—not by a long shot. By exploiting rich monasteries for prebends[19] owed to them, cardinals were awash in luxury, Luther observed. Furthermore, the generally immoral behavior—especially among the clergy—repulsed him.

Nevertheless, to a certain extent Rome had captured Luther's heart, and he eagerly did the classic "pilgrimage tour." This included pilgrimages to each of Rome's seven main churches in a single day, beginning outside of the gates of Rome at the Church of St. Paul, where the remains of the apostle Paul are entombed. Next, there was the Church of St. Sebastian along the Via Appia, then the Basilica of St. John Lateran, the Church of

Pilgrims on the steps of the Lateran Palace.

the Holy Cross, the Church of St. Lawrence, St. Maria Maggiore, and, finally, the Basilica of St. Peter, where a Mass was celebrated. Because they knew they would be attending Mass that evening, every pilgrim on the tour had to fast all day long. Luther also went on pilgrimages to other churches and catacombs, took in all the history, and read a Mass wherever possible.

Without any concern for his trousers—he considered the Italian styles to be more elegant—Luther crawled up the steps to

Sights in Rome: The Basilica of St. Peter

The Basilica of St. Peter is a good example of the many sights in Rome. During Luther's sojourn there, Pope Julius II (1443–1513) ordered the new basilica to be built and the oldest church in Rome, the Church of St. Peter, to be demolished. It was during the same period that Michelangelo painted the ceiling of the Sistine Chapel and that Raphael decorated the private chambers of the pope with frescos.

the Palace of Pilate in the Lateran Palace, praying the Lord's Prayer on every step. He did all of this to free his grandfather from purgatory. But as soon as he had reached the top step, Luther already began to doubt whether all his efforts had been worthwhile. His attempt to resolve the conflict of the order was equally unsuccessful. Thus, in the winter of 1511, Luther returned to Erfurt without having accomplished anything.

The Tower Experience

To be sure, I was unusually zealous in trying to understand Paul in his Epistle to the Romans. But there was one little phrase in chapter 1 with which I struggled. It was the phrase: "in it[20] the righteousness of God is revealed." I hated the phrase "the righteousness of God" because I had been taught . . . to understand "righteousness" . . . in the sense that God is just and therefore punishes sinners and the unjust. Even though I was living as a blameless monk, I felt that before God I was still a sinner with an uneasy conscience. I could not rely on being justified by making my own amends. I was not able to love this "just" God. In fact, I hated Him because He punishes sinners. When I did not blaspheme out loud, I certainly expressed my outrage at God with vicious murmuring: "As though it were not quite enough to oppress and afflict us miserable sinners, who are already eternally lost because of original sin, with but one law of the Ten Commandments! On top of this, with the Gospel He has now added fresh pain to our old pain! Even with the Gospel, God is threatening us with His righteous anger!" This caused me to rage, driven by a wild and confused conscience. I ruthlessly kept on beating my head against that particular passage of Paul's. I was hungry and thirsty to find out what St. Paul was trying to say.[21]

Finally, God showed me mercy. After wracking my brains for days, I suddenly noticed the correlation of the words in the verse: "For in it the righteousness of God is revealed from faith for faith, as it is written, 'The righteous shall live by faith.'"[22] At that point I began to understand the righteousness of God: namely, that the person who is

In the tower room of the Augustinian Monastery of Wittenberg, Luther finally grasped the meaning of "faith."

justified because of a gift of God lives by it and, in fact, by faith.[23] At that point, I felt as if I were completely born again. I felt like I had stepped through an open gate into paradise. Suddenly, all of Scripture opened itself up to me seamlessly in a brand-new light. I ran through Scripture by memory and discovered the same concept in other passages: God's work consists in what He works in us. God's power consists in His making us powerful. God's wisdom consists in His making us wise. The same is true for the strength of God, the salvation of God, and the honor of God. Now, as much as I used to hate the righteousness of God, I now lifted up this sweetest of words in my love. In this way, this passage of Paul became the gate to paradise for me.[24]

Today, this insight of Luther, which occurred in his study in the tower of Wittenberg's Augustinian Monastery (today called Luther House), is known as the "Tower Experience." Luther's study of the Bible triggered this insight, and it is regarded as the start of the Reformation. What this means for believers is that God's Word reveals that they are sinners but that they are declared righteous by the Gospel without meeting any requirement. In that way, the just God is also the merciful God in Christ.

Luther's Rose—The Seal of Luther

On July 8, 1530, Luther wrote the following words to Lazarus Spengler regarding the "Luther Rose":

> Because you inquired as to whether my seal has "hit the mark" or not, I would like to share my original thoughts with you. . . . I have summarized them in a seal that illustrates my theology. First, we have a black cross lying on a heart that should be its natural color. This reminds me personally that it is only faith in the Crucified One that saves us. For if you believe from your heart, you will be justified. Although that cross is black—that is, even though it kills and is supposed to hurt—the heart retains its natural color. This means that the cross does not destroy the heart's nature. In other words, the cross does not kill, but keeps alive. *Iustus enim fide vivet, sed fide crucifixi* ["For the righteous shall live by faith, yet faith in the Crucified One"]. This heart is at the center of a white rose. This shows that faith gives joy, consolation, and peace and quickly forms a joyful white rose, [but] not the way the world gives peace and joy. For this reason, the rose should be white and not red, because white is the color of the spirits and all angels. This rose is in a sky blue field because joy in spirit and faith is the beginning of the future, even though our heavenly joy is not yet complete. This joy is captured by hope, yet that joy is not yet manifest. And [I place] a gold ring in that field [as a sign] that this blessedness is eternal in heaven and that it is more precious than all joy and possessions, just as gold is the highest, most precious metal.[25]

In its Market Square (*Marktplatz*), the city of Luther honors the reformer with this impressive Luther statue, designed by Gottfried Schadow in 1821.

CHAPTER FIVE

Wittenberg—City of the Reformation

With its formerly remote location, Wittenberg at first appeared to have torn Luther away from mainstream events. Yet it was precisely Wittenberg's new spiritual and social environment that triggered the opposite with him. Supported by his colleagues at the newly founded University of Wittenberg, Luther was now in a position to unleash monumental forces, as today's historians recognize.

Wittenberg in the Late Middle Ages

Wittenberg was first documented in 1180 as *burchwardum wittenburg*, and from 1200 on, it belonged to the ruling Ascanians. In 1260, Albrecht II established his residence there, and in 1293 he gave Wittenberg the rights of a city. In 1356, Wittenberg became the residence of the elector and had a high court beginning in 1441. Located in an agricultural setting, Wittenberg at that time was known only as a regional trade center for shoemakers, cloth makers, butchers, and bakers.

Of the 356 home owners paying property tax, 172 had the right to brew beer. The remaining 184 residents were so-called *Buddelinge*, owning tiny homes. Wittenberg was fortified with eleven towers, which have been preserved to this day. They remain situated around its three gated towers: the Elbe Gate to the south, the Coswig Gate (also known as the Castle Gate) to the west, and the Elster Gate to the east. Today, the Collegienstrasse and Coswiger Strasse are the city's main streets. The highest points in the Old Town are both the Market Square (*Marktplatz*) and the Church Square (*Kirchplatz*).

Wittenberg's main structures are its city hall (*Rathaus*) and the Parish Church of St. Mary, which was expanded in the fifteenth century and was the church that Luther served as preaching pastor.

Wittenberg City Hall.

Wittenberg University

In 1502, Elector Frederick III, also known as Frederick the Wise, founded the Leucorea University of Electoral Saxony (*leukos* means "white" and refers to "Wittenberg," that is, "white mountain"). Permission to found the university had been granted by Emperor Maximilian, and the university celebrated its opening on October 18, 1502.

In the early thirteenth century, universities had been founded elsewhere under the authority and supervision of the pope. These universities taught the Aristotelian academic methods customary in the Middle Ages, as well as the cultivation of Roman law in the area of jurisprudence. But over time, secular powers (kings, princes, and cities) began to found universities, blending the concepts of the Late Middle Ages with recently emerging humanistic ideas. Nontheological subjects were beginning to grow in their independence and significance. This was also the case at the Leucorea, which Frederick had founded mainly in the hope of improving the administration of his princedom.

In those years, there was still a decidedly medieval aura to the Leucorea, however, because St. Augustine was chosen as its patron saint. Furthermore, each department was appointed its own patron saint. To determine the correct seating order at staff meetings, the various faculties were ranked. As was customary in the Late Middle Ages, the theological department sat at the head of the table, followed by the law and medical faculties in less prominent positions. At the bottom of the ranking was the arts faculty, which taught the seven liberal arts as prerequisite studies.

One new regulation, however, indicated the spirit of rising humanism in that era: crowned poets (*poetae laureati*) were now ranked with the masters of the arts faculty. These poets represented German humanism. As such, they dealt with the ancient languages—Greek, Latin, and Hebrew, plus their respective literature—in new ways and also especially devoted themselves to rhetoric. New faculty positions for the humanities were also being created at the university.

The northern courtyard of the Leucorea building in "Luther City," Wittenberg.

The university required a large amount of teaching materials for its students, especially in the humanities. Thus printers moved into town, and Wittenberg's first printed texts were made available the same year the university was founded. In this way, the university contributed significantly to the economic boom of Wittenberg.

Frederick the Wise assigned two Augustinian hermits as professors. One position was in the theological faculty. The second position was in the arts faculty, giving lectures on moral philosophy. The prior of the Augustinian Monastery, Johann von Staupitz, who cofounded the Leucorea, required these Augustinian hermits to take general studies themselves. This guaranteed that they would attend every academic event.

Frederick the Wise also increased the number of canon regulars at the university to twelve and made attendance at the lectures mandatory for them as well. This at least partially ensured the salary of the professors.[26] In light of these transitions, the

Castle Church also became the university church. Elections for the various university offices were held in the sacristy, while the sanctuary served as the main hall of the Leucorea.

With professors and students moving into town, the economy of the city picked up even more, which is why the city of Wittenberg supported the Leucorea as much as possible. For instance, the confession house at the Franciscan Monastery was arranged so the arts faculty would be able to use it as a lecture hall. New seating was acquired for the City Church so university festivities could be held there until the Castle Church was completed.

Construction of the Leucorea also triggered changes in Wittenberg's municipal planning. Because student accommodations had not yet been completed—and even after their completion would not be able to house all the students—some students had to live in private homes in Wittenberg. To address this housing shortage, a law was passed in 1504 that anyone owning or inheriting a lot without a structure on it had to build a structure on that property within one year. In this way, the Leucorea triggered Wittenberg's first building boom of the sixteenth century. Buildings were constructed on vacant lots, homes were expanded to include small businesses for craftsmen or merchants, and other buildings were constructed as well. Even professors took in students, as did Luther and his wife, Katharina. This is when the houses now located around the City Church were built, separating the church from the city hall.[27]

Securing the water supply for so many people was now becoming increasingly difficult. At that time, the only water supply was from streams that had been diverted into town and from which people drew their drinking water. But these streams also were for the disposal of raw sewage, which then flowed into the Elbe River.[28] Beer brewers were beginning to complain about the poor water quality, and the few wells that had been dug were not providing enough water. For this reason, in 1542 Elector John Frederick commissioned Mayor Philipp Reichenbach and District Magistrate Christoph Gross to construct a system of piped water, which would supply the elector's castle and the fortress of Wittenberg with sufficient water.

Yet the citizens did not want to be dependent on the elector and wanted piped water too. Thus in 1556 seven Wittenberg businessmen formed a group, had a well dug in the area of the Bruder-Annendorfer-Mark, and had water piped into their homes in wooden pipes. Some of this medieval plumbing can still be seen today.

Wittenberg Castle and the Castle Church

As early as 1490, Wittenberg was of key interest for the electors, beginning with Elector Frederick the Wise, who had the castle built. The former castle of the Ascanians had been torn down, and in 1509 the new castle with two wings was completed. According to records, construction costs were 32,466 guilders, 13 groschen, and nine pfennigs. This new construction was made complete by the Castle Church, which was new and formed the third wing of the residential castle. The Castle Church also served as the church of the *Allerheiligenstift* (a collegiate church), and, from 1503 on, it officially served as the university church as well. For this reason, its door was used as a "bulletin board" for academic theses.

The *Allerheiligenstift* had been built in 1346. In addition to a provost's position, it had six canon prebends[29] and priceless relics,[30] including a thorn from Christ's crown of thorns. A collector for many years, Frederick the Wise had expanded the castle's existing treasury of relics. Such piety was typical for the Late Middle Ages. The canon also granted special indulgences, such as the so-called *portiuncula* indulgence of St. Francis of Assisi. Granting forgiveness for sins that had not yet been committed, this indulgence could normally be purchased only in the chapel of St. Francis in Assisi.

The Castle Church was richly appointed, with a high altar painted by Lucas Cranach the Elder. Some of its seventeen known paintings are preserved, though not all are in the Castle Church today. One of Cranach's works still hanging in the Castle Church is the Martyrdom of St. Catherine. On the side wings there were depictions of six female saints known as the "Princes' Altar of Dessau" (*Dessauer Fürstenaltar*). Today this painting is exhibited in Dessau's Georgium Castle in the Anhalt Art Gallery (*Anhaltischen Gemäldegalerie*). World-famous painter Albrecht Dürer contributed some of the works that were originally in the Castle Church, of which four are preserved. Two panels depict the "Seven Joys of the Virgin Altarpiece" and the "Seven Sorrows of the Virgin." The panel depicting the seven sorrows is now in Dresden, while the depiction of the Virgin is displayed in the Alte Pinakothek in Munich.

By continuously sponsoring Masses, the elector filled the church with life—life he still considered spiritual at that time. Thus in one year 1,138 Masses were sung and 7,856 Masses were read. In the liturgy of the hours, 40,932 candles were lit. The wax of these candles weighed more than 66 hundredweights.

The Castle Church in Wittenberg.

When Frederick the Wise died, the Castle Church lost its importance. His brother who succeeded him, John the Steadfast, positioned himself more clearly on the side of the Reformation and closed the *Allerheiligenstift* in 1525. Under a cloud of secrecy, the huge collection of relics was brought to Torgau. Georg Goldschmidt separated the gold, silver, jewels, and pearls they contained and reworked them into items of daily use. The silver was then sold to Nuremberg, with a profit of 24,739 guilders, which was used to support the court.[31] A few items were preserved, however, such as a drinking glass owned by Elisabeth of Thuringia, which presumably came from a crusade. Today it can be viewed in Coburg Castle (*Veste Coburg*).

In 1760, the Castle Church and its rich furnishings were destroyed. Sadly, the only items from inside the original church that survived were the tomb figures of Frederick the Wise and his brother, John the Steadfast.

In 1892, the church was renovated in the neo-Gothic style. Statues commemorating Luther and his most important allies were placed in the interior on both sides of the aisle: Justus Jonas, Johannes Bugenhagen, Nikolaus von Amsdorf, Urbanus Rhegius, Georg Spalatin, Philipp Melanchthon, Johannes Brenz, and Caspar Cruciger. On the ceiling you can see the seals of the towns that sided with the Reformation. Of the original 198 seals, 128 are preserved. On the walls are the coats of arms of the reformers.

The pulpit shows the four Gospel writers, plus additional coats of arms of the cities that played a major role in Luther's life: Eisleben, Erfurt, Wittenberg, and Worms.

The balcony displays fifty-two coats of arms of the noblemen who dealt with Luther during the first half of the sixteenth century. This rich collection of coats of arms illustrates the intention of crown prince Frederick William III (who later became Emperor Frederick III) to embellish the Castle Church as a "sanctuary for all of Protestant Christianity." The only features of the Renaissance-era castle that remain today are the magnificent stairwells, which lead into nothingness. This is because the original building had three stories, but a fourth was added when the church was transformed into a Prussian fortress.

Luther's House

The focal point of Luther's private and professional life was the former Augustinian Monastery. Referring to the black cowls its resident monks wore, it was also known as the Black Abbey. It was located near the Elster Gate, south of the city wall, where the Holy Ghost Hospital (*Heilig-Geist-Spital*) was originally located.

Johann von Staupitz had founded the monastery in 1502 when the university was built, though he was not able to complete the monastery as originally planned to include a church and cloistered courtyard. He did, however, have the building expanded into a monastic house with lecture halls for the university on the second floor and accommodations for about forty monks on the third floor. At any point in time, some fifteen to twenty monks from out of town lived here while attending the university.

Luther lived in this monastery for a while, too, though he probably did his reading and writing in the dining room in the evening, where Cranach's Ten Commandments panel can be viewed today. Later, Luther and his family lived on the second floor, but because of countless renovations over the centuries, we no longer have the exact floor plan.

Naturally, Luther's large home with its numerous occupants could not be run without servants. Luther had his own servant, Wolf Seberger, who received a small salary from the elector. Luther frequently had to send the elector a reminder to continue paying the servant's salary. Seberger was responsible for purchasing supplies, tending the garden, and running the household business. Luther regarded him as good-natured but often complained about his laziness.

In addition to Luther House, Luther and his wife also ran a small farm, Zülsdorf, which was probably purchased primarily because Katharina wanted it.[32] Apparently it had once belonged to her family. The farm was well run and provided food for the Luther household.

Luther's "Katie" sometimes also received gifts from friends, such as fish, game, wine, and beer. However, shortages occasionally forced Luther to go without beer—once even for a period of forty days in the summer of 1540, when barley and hops were not available.

But that could not make Luther angry. What did make him angry toward the end of his life, however, was the way many people despised God's Word. This attitude in turn led to immoral behavior among the population, which became obvious in the way the women of Wittenberg wore dresses that were too short and too low in the neck. For that reason, Luther wrote to Katie on July 28, 1545, from the town of Zeitz:

> To my dear wife and manager of our household, Katharina von Bora—"preacher," beer brewer, gardener, and whatever else you may be—grace and peace. Dear Katie, [our son] Hans will tell you all about our trip. . . . I wish I could avoid returning to Wittenberg. My heart has grown so cold that I no longer enjoy being there. I would like you to sell our garden and plot, our house and yard. Also, I would like to return that big house to my dearest lord, the elector. It would be best for you to move to Zülsdorf while I am alive. I imagine my salary would help you to improve our little farm. . . . I cannot believe how women—both old and young—in Wittenberg are starting to expose themselves in front and in back and that there is no one around who would punish them or try to prevent this behavior! By doing that, God's Word is scorned.[33]

Luther did not return to Wittenberg until the elector, the city, and the university promised to address the situation.[34]

Clothing in Luther's Day

Portrait of a Woman
(ca. 1480).

Even before the Reformation era, clothing indicated one's social status. Only the high aristocracy could afford expensive colors, such as purple (from a snail known as the spiny dye-murex) or carmine (from insects). This was also true for certain decorations and rare materials, such as silk. The lower classes wore linen, hemp, untreated cotton, or sheep's wool. These materials sometimes were dyed with natural colors extracted from plants.

Farmers and day laborers usually made their own clothing, while the nobility or clerics purchased their clothes with money gained from taxes.

In the Middle Ages, men wore linen underwear covered by wool cloaks and fastened with a belt. Over this they wore a square cloak, which was fastened on the right side with a clasp. Men also wore felt hats and kept their legs warm with long stockings pulled above shoes made from sewn leather.

Women wore long linen undergarments with long sleeves over which an ankle-length outer garment was worn. Over this was worn a cape that closed over the chest. Women's head coverings were made from linen and were about three to six centimeters (one to almost three inches) wide; on top of these were placed small, flat bonnets or veils.

Noble women wore richly decorated turbanlike head coverings. Shoes were pointed and made from soft, decorated leather. As had been the fashion in Roman times, women often bleached their hair blonde.

Over the course of time, fashions differentiated according to regions. For instance, beginning in the fifteenth century, townspeople wore shoes with wooden soles, which protected their feet from mud and moisture.

Luther complained about the general obsession of both the rich and the poor with their clothing:

> Do we not all know endless stories about how much time and money people spend on their clothing? Therefore, it should no longer be called simply a desire or an overindulgence, but rather foolishness for them to adorn themselves with so much clothing and jewelry—like donkeys that are born to lug around gold.[35]

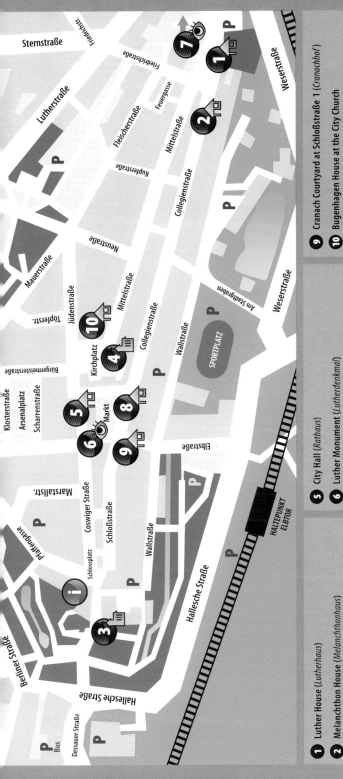

1 Luther House (*Lutherhaus*)

2 Melanchthon House (*Melanchthonhaus*)

3 Castle Church with Theses door (*Schlosskirche mit der Thesentür*)

4 City Church of St. Mary (*Stadtkirche St. Marien*)

5 City Hall (*Rathaus*)

6 Luther Monument (*Lutherdenkmal*)

7 Luther's Oak Tree (*Luthereiche*)

8 Cranach House at Markt 3–4 (*Cranachhaus*)

9 Cranach Courtyard at Schloßstraße 1 (*Cranachhof*)

10 Bugenhagen House at the City Church (*Bugenhagenhaus an der Stadtkirche*)

i Information

Map labels: Sternstraße, Friedrichstr., Lutherstraße, Friedrichstraße, Fleischerstraße, Feuergasse, Mittelstraße, Kupferstraße, Collegienstraße, Mauerstraße, Neustraße, Weserstraße, Jüdenstraße, Töpferstr., Mittelstraße, Burgermeisterstraße, Kirchplatz, Collegienstraße, Wallstraße, Klosterstraße, Arsenalplatz, Scharrenstraße, Markt, Am Stadtgraben, SPORTPLATZ, Wallstraße, Weserstraße, Marstallstr., Coswiger Straße, Schloßstraße, Elbstraße, Pfaffengasse, Schlossplatz, Wallstraße, Hallesche Straße, HALTEPUNKT ELBTOR, Berliner Straße, Dessauer Straße, Hallesche Straße, P Bus, P

Sights in Wittenberg

Luther House (*Lutherhaus*)

Beginning in 1508, the reformer lived in this building. Katharina von Bora moved in when they were married in 1525. Luther House was converted into a museum in 1883 (for a picture of it, see "The Tower Experience" on page 35).

Melanchthon House (*Melanchthonhaus*)

Located on Collegienstrasse, the home was purchased by Philipp Melanchthon in 1520 at the time of his wedding. After a number of years, the house began to fall apart, so Elector John Frederick gave Melanchthon a new house in 1536. This Renaissance-era building is now a museum.

Castle Church with Ninety-five Theses Door (*Schlosskirche*)

According to tradition, it is here that Luther posted his Ninety-five Theses. Since that original door was destroyed in the Seven Years' War, this historic act was memorialized in 1858 by a new bronze "Theses Door." Luther often preached in the Castle Church, especially when the electoral court was in town.

City Church of St. Mary (*Stadtkirche St. Marien*)

It is here where reformers Martin Luther and Johannes Bugenhagen preached most frequently. This is also the church in which the first Mass was held in the German language and in which the Lord's Supper was first administered to the congregation in "both kinds," that is, with both bread and wine. For this reason, the church is considered to be the "mother church" of the Reformation.

The City Church of St. Mary was first documented in 1187. The chancel and southern nave were added in 1280. Additional enhancements were made in the fifteenth century. As a result of the iconoclasm triggered by Andreas Bodenstein,[36] almost the entire interior was destroyed. Seeking to prevent further damage, Luther returned from the Wartburg and delivered his famous Invocavit sermons here.

Along with the ensuing expansions of 1280, a so-called "Jewish Sow" (*Judensau*) was affixed on the south-eastern corner.[37] Such was the case with several other churches in Europe as well. Its purpose was not to depict or warn against Jews—since Jesus and His disciples were, of course, all Jewish themselves—but against their spiritual food, namely, the Talmud, which opposes Christ.[38]

After several years of discussion about allowing the infamous "Jewish Sow" to remain, on November 11, 1988, another plaster monument was unveiled beneath the already existing

monument. It is meant to communicate to Jews that Christians do not deny their own guilty past. The text reads: "God's real name,[39] / the despised Shem Hamphoras, / which Jews even before Christians / regarded as almost unspeakable, / died with six million Jews / under the sign of the cross."[40] Below this statement is a quote in Hebrew from Psalm 130: "Out of the depths I cry to you, O Lord!"

City Hall (*Rathaus*)

During the Reformation, Wittenberg prospered and its population grew. Soon the town outgrew the old city hall, and beginning in 1523 (and thus even in Luther's day), it was expanded and renovated until it took on its current dimensions.

Legal decisions were rendered outside the main door, and executions were carried out in front of the portal. A closer look at the cobblestoned market square in front of the city hall reveals traces of where the gallows once stood. After proclamation of the sentence, the "poor sinner's bell" was rung. It sounded for the last time on May 9, 1834, when a butcher's apprentice named Ernst Wollkopf was convicted of murder and broken on the wheel.

While Cranach discharged his duties as mayor for many years, Wittenberg's city hall also served other purposes as well. For instance, the cellar once contained a tavern (*Ratskeller*) as well as a jail, and cloth makers and shoemakers at one point sold their products in the public marketplace (*Bürgersaal*).[41]

Luther Monument (*Lutherdenkmal*)

Designed by Johann Gottfried Schadow, Wittenberg's Luther Monument is one of the largest bronze statues. It was presented to the citizens in 1821, a very early date for a Luther monument. In comparison, it was not until 1883 that

Eisleben erected a Luther monument for the 400th anniversary of the reformer's birth. The Eisleben monument was designed by Rudolf Siemering.[42]

Luther's Oak (*Luthereiche*)

This tree was planted in memory of December 10, 1520, the date on which Luther burned the papal bull threatening excommunication. It stands on the corner of Lutherstrasse and Dresdener Strasse. The original tree planted at this site no longer exists. The tree currently at the site was planted in 1830.

Cranach House at Markt 3–4 (*Cranachhaus*)

In 1505, Cranach was called to Wittenberg. He first lived in the Painter's Room (*Malerstube*) in the castle. He probably married in 1512, bought the properties at Markt 3–4, and moved there that same year.[43]

Cranach Courtyard at Schloßstrasse 1 (*Cranachhof*)

Cranach purchased the largest building complex in Wittenberg when his work had outgrown the studio at the Markt—a clear testimony of his success as a painter.

Bugenhagen House near the City Church (*Bugenhagenhaus*)

This building was once the parsonage of St. Mary's. Luther's fellow reformer, Johannes Bugenhagen, lived here until his death in 1558.

Katharina von Bora, portrait by Lucas Cranach the Elder
(after 1528).

CHAPTER SIX

Wittenberg—Place of Meeting

Katharina von Bora

Not only was Wittenberg the town where Luther would meet key people in his life, it was also where he would marry Katharina von Bora. In 1531, he praised the virtues of his wife:

> I would not trade my Katie for both France and Venice. First, because God gave her to me, and He gave me to her; second, because I often notice that other women have more faults than she does (though she has a few of her own, she has many great virtues offsetting them); third, because she keeps the *fides matrimonii*, that is, the faith and honor of marriage. In the same way, a wife should think that about her husband too.[44]

The wedding of Luther and Katharina von Bora in 1525 surprised friend and foe alike. But there is a backstory to their wedding.

Luther's criticism of the practice of celibacy and of monastic vows had already prompted a wave of priests to marry and had caused monks and nuns to leave their monasteries. While still single and living in a monastery, Luther supported people who had fled from other cloistered groups.

On April 7, 1523, twelve nuns hidden in herring barrels escaped from the abbey at Nimbschen, near Grimma. Nine of these women came to Wittenberg. Luther sympathized with their escape and tried to find places for them to stay. His efforts were successful for eight of them, but he was unable to find a place for the ninth—a nun named Katharina von Bora—because she kept turning down various offers. Finally, she suggested that Luther and she should marry.

In defiance of the dangers of the Peasants' War, Luther intended his marriage to be a sign of faith in God. In this way, Luther wanted to "practice what he had been preaching" about the objectionable nature of celibacy.

Melanchthon, on the other hand, thought the timing of Luther's marriage was disastrous because the Peasants' War required that Luther exhibit complete authority. Melanchthon supposed that Katharina had beguiled Luther. Furthermore, Melanchthon was upset that Luther had not confided to him his plans to marry.

Some contemporaries repeated an old legend that a marriage between a monk and a nun would beget the Antichrist. On the other hand, illustrations from Luther's New Testament and "Against the Execrable Bull of the Antichrist" (a Luther writing from five years earlier) had already been teaching the people of Electoral Saxony who should be regarded as the Antichrist: the author of the bull excommunicating Luther from the Church. Needless to say, Katharina shared this opinion too.

After the wedding, Frederick the Wise gave Luther the salary of a professor as well as the Augustinian Monastery in which to live. To be sure, the condition of the building was deplorable. To make matters worse, the newlyweds did not own many household goods because monks leaving the monastery typically returned to the world with not much more than the clothes on their backs. In fact, Luther's straw bed had not been aired out properly by his negligent servant, so it was molding from being dampened by sweat.[45]

Over time, Katharina managed to turn the former monastery into the Luther House. To supplement the family income, she turned some of the rooms into student housing. In this way, theology and family life were closely intertwined in Luther's home. On June 7, 1526, Hans, their first child, was born. Other children followed. In fact, before long, Martin Luther, Katharina von Bora, and their children became symbols for a new middle-class Christianity and a role model for other pastors' families.

Katharina von Bora came from a noble family that had hit on hard times. But thanks to her years in the abbey, she had received an education that surpassed that of most other women of her era. Luther allowed her to retain her maiden name, which kept the memory of her noble ancestry alive.

The way Luther addressed Katharina in his letters documents how much he loved and honored his wife.[46] This is also apparent from his last will, in which he names her as his heiress—something quite unusual in those days. Much to her dismay, however, Gregor Brück, the elector's chancellor, would not recognize her as an heiress.

Luther's Children

While Luther does not share much about his children in his writings, he did care about them. He sent them letters, gave them presents, and described them as the greatest joy of their parents.

Luther had his children privately tutored by his students. For whatever reason, he was particularly strict with his oldest son, Hans, but was not as stern with the younger children.

Luther's unreasonably high expectations for Hans inevitably led to disappointments. Enrolled at the university in 1533 at the age of seven, Hans completed the bachelor's degree exam in 1539. He was then sent to a good school in Torgau, together with his cousin Florian von Bora. Hans suffered from being far away

Luther and Education

Luther had noticed that the numbers of pupils and students had decreased after the boom of the Reformation and humanism. Believing that the school system was going downhill, this is what Luther at one point wrote to the city councilmen:

> I think that in the sight of God no outward sin so heavily burdens the world and merits such severe punishment as this very sin which we commit against children by not educating them.[47]

Miniature portrait to the Gospel of St. Matthew.

In the preface to this writing, Luther emphasizes that it is God's command for the secular authorities to take on the duty of educating. Luther gives a theological reason for this demand: the goal of all academics—especially of the study of language, literature, and grammar—is to interpret Holy Scripture.

Naturally, in his writings Luther pre-supposes the form of government of his day and age. But his insight remains valid: education and training are necessary for the formation of new generations of competent politicians and citizens who will be capable of making responsible decisions. For this reason, Luther is adamant that boys and girls attend school.

and experienced homesickness, but recalling his own school days, Luther insisted that Hans stick it out and learn to deal with the separation. The only time Hans was allowed to return to Wittenberg was when his sister Magdalene became ill.

Luther was preparing his daughter for the possibility that God might be calling her to Himself. She was without fear, and on September 20, 1542, she died in Luther's arms.

Children were not the only people living in the Luther home; relatives on both sides resided there as well. Magdalena von Bora, an aunt of Katharina's who was also called "Muhme Lene," stayed with them until her death in 1537. Furthermore, Luther and Katharina took in the four children of Luther's deceased sister, two of his nephews, and a niece of Katharina's. Of course, the size of this family often led to commotion, and Katharina did not always have it easy. Luther himself thought his family needed the strict discipline customary among the Turks.

Driven by a deep sense of family, Luther helped select spouses for his nieces and nephews. He sometimes even took in distant relatives and poor people.

At times, swindlers and con artists abused Luther's kindness, which forced him to become more careful in his later years. Nevertheless, even as late as 1541,[48] Luther threw out a "filthy whore"[49] who had wormed her way in and abused the family's trust. She had introduced herself as Rosina von

Truchsess, claiming to be an escaped nun. But it turned out she was pregnant and had attempted to abort her child.[50] Finally, she maintained she was a poor orphan, the daughter of a rebel who had been executed. It is said that she then moved on to other parishes, where she continued to lie and steal.

Elector Frederick the Wise

In 1486, Frederick III became the elector of Saxony at the age of twenty-three. Promoting the new education movement, he was in touch with humanist Johannes Reuchlin, who recommended the appointment of Philipp Melanchthon. The elector also took advice from Erasmus of Rotterdam. A friend of the fine arts, Frederick commissioned many of the best artists.

As mentioned in the section on his collection of relics, Frederick's piety was typical for the Late Middle Ages. As such, he even went on a pilgrimage to the Holy Land. Although he never married, he and his mistress had three children.

On the political scene, the new elector played his part skillfully. From an ecclesiastical point of view, the region of Electoral Saxony belonged to several bishoprics, namely, Meissen, Naumburg, Mainz, Halberstadt, Magdeburg, Brandenburg, Bamberg, and Würzburg. The fact that all these various entities could not agree on a variety of issues helped to strengthen the position of the secular rulers. Furthermore, the two churches of the *Allerheiligenstift* (see above) reported directly to the pope and thus could not be touched by the bishop of Brandenburg.

For personal and political reasons, Frederick was interested in modernizing the churches in his territory. He was convinced that reforms were overdue and that the asserted demands for the removal of abuses were legitimate. On its own, the Church would hardly be able to make these changes, he thought, which is why Frederick supported Luther's attempts to reform the

Church. Although Luther spent much time in Torgau, the two men never met face-to-face.[51]

This is Frederick the Wise's attitude toward Martin Luther, whom he continually protected:

> Whenever he was asked why he let Dr. Luther remain in his territory, Duke Frederick would wisely say, "I do not know anything bad about him. I have nothing to do with him. If he does anything wrong, then discuss the matter with him in Wittenberg where I have a university. He should be answerable to you. I have so many learned people in Wittenberg! If he did anything wrong, they would not tolerate him."[52]

Melanchthon

Melanchthon came to Wittenberg at an early age. Born in 1497 as the son of Georg Schwarzerdt (which means "black earth" in German), Melanchthon (the Greek rendering of his last name) enrolled at the University of Heidelberg in 1509. He transferred to Tübingen in 1512, earned a master's degree, and was a professor there from 1514 to 1518. He remained a professor his whole life.

The newly founded Wittenberg University turned to the well-known Johannes Reuchlin to fill its teaching position for Greek. He recommended his grandnephew, Melanchthon, who accepted the call. Melanchthon arrived in Wittenberg on August 25, 1518.

From the outset, Melanchthon was completely successful as a lecturer. Five to six hundred listeners would crowd into his lecture hall. On his part, Melanchthon saw in Luther the embodiment of true, Christian godliness.

In his August 29, 1518, opening lecture, which addressed university reforms, the twenty-one-year-old succeeded in winning the hearts of his audience.

In collaboration with the other faculty members, Melanchthon started to reform the university in accordance with the wishes of Frederick the Wise. Luther was pleased to have Melanchthon in Wittenberg, and the two men became close friends, both professionally and personally, even though their personalities were entirely different. Melanchthon was timid, sometimes insecure, and sensitive, but he was surrounded by Luther, who looked after him. In Wittenberg they lived close to each other, and their back doors were connected by a footpath, so they could visit with each other at any time without being seen from the street.

Melanchthon's first years in Wittenberg were characterized by his acceptance of Lutheran theology. He also explained this in his lectures.

Melanchthon bore the brunt of the responsibility of the so-called "Wittenberg Unrest" during Luther's stay at the Wartburg, but he did not feel up to the challenges that ensued from it. Once Luther returned, therefore, Melanchthon handed over more and more of the Reformation work to Luther so he could concentrate again on his area of expertise, that is, the reformation of the education system. This is how Melanchthon acquired his nickname, "Praeceptor Germaniae," that is, the "Teacher of Germany." His reforms at the University of Wittenberg became a role model for many other universities. Beyond that, he provided substantial impetus for the educational system in general.[53]

Spalatin

Johannes Spalatin was named after the town of his birth, Spalt (near Nuremberg), where he was born as Johannes Burckhardt on January 17, 1484.

Spalatin studied at Erfurt and Wittenberg and became part of the court of Electoral Saxony in 1509. Initially working as a librarian and an archivist, Spalatin advanced to the positions of secretary, privy councilor, and court preacher. Spalatin was the intermediary between Luther and Frederick the Wise, which is evident from the more than four hundred letters from Luther to Spalatin that have been preserved.

Spalatin met Luther early on in Wittenberg, and before he became Luther's "mouthpiece" to the elector, Spalatin was Luther's theological mentor. A careful and thoughtful man, Spalatin encouraged the elector, who was even more careful than Spalatin himself, to support Luther and to remain true to the reformer.

After Frederick died, Spalatin became the pastor in Altenburg, where he was able to implement the Reformation despite great difficulties. Nonetheless, Spalatin was continually an official delegate at a number of key events: in 1526, at the Imperial Diet in Speyer; in 1530, in Augsburg; and in 1537, in Smalcald (*Schmalkalden*). In addition to his contributions to the Reformation, Spalatin's translations and historical writings are of great importance.

Johann von Staupitz

Born in 1468, Johann von Staupitz was an Augustinian hermit. After studies in Cologne and Leipzig, he presumably joined the Augustinian Monastery in Munich. He began his studies of theology in 1497 in Tübingen, while serving as prior of the monastery in that town. He received his doctorate in theology in 1500.

As previously mentioned, Frederick, the elector of Saxony, who had known Staupitz from his youth, called him in 1502 from the monastery in Munich to Wittenberg to help build the university, which had been founded along with Wittenberg's Augustinian Monastery. In Tübingen, Staupitz had experienced a close working relationship between a mendicant order and a university. He applied this model to Wittenberg, where in 1502 he took on the professorship of Scripture and became the first dean of the theological faculty. When he laid down his post in 1512, he was succeeded by Luther. During Luther's years as a monk, Staupitz had served as Luther's pastor and consoled him in his struggles of conscience.

Lucas Cranach the Elder

Even today, when people think of Luther, in their mind's eye they are probably visualizing one of Cranach the Elder's paintings. Almost every portrait of Luther existing to this day is a painting by Cranach.

Cranach did his first paintings of the reformer in 1520. At that time, Luther was already the godfather of Cranach's youngest daughter—proof that the two men were connected not only professionally but also personally. Around this time, Cranach worked on a copper engraving depicting Luther as a monk, wearing his doctoral hat. In December 1521, Luther traveled in disguise from the Wartburg to Wittenberg and had Cranach do the woodcut of "Junker Jörg."

One of their greatest joint ventures was the printing of the New Testament, which Luther had translated while at the Wartburg. After five months of preparatory work, the New Testament was published just before September 25, 1522.[54] It included twenty-one full-page woodcuts by Cranach. Because it was published in September, this edition is also known as the "September Testament." Despite five thousand copies produced in the first printing, it quickly sold out. The second edition (the "December Testament") followed three months later. By 1534, seventeen printings had been done in Wittenberg alone.

Each copy cost ten and a half groschen, whereas the bound form probably cost one guilder (about the price of a pig ready for slaughter). As a matter of principle, Luther would not accept an honorarium, which meant a huge profit for Cranach. During this period, Cranach also ventured into the book-selling trade. He opened a bookstore, which was located in his home at Marktplatz 3 until 1533.

Cranach's financial success went hand in hand with his advancement in Wittenberg's social circles. He served on Wittenberg's city council for thirty years—from 1519 to 1549. However, the council's regulations stated that one third of the twenty-one councilmen could govern for only one year each triennium, so in reality Cranach governed for only ten years. Cranach also served as chamberlain three times and as mayor in 1537, 1540, and 1543.

Cranach is generally known as the person who put Luther's thoughts into pictures. An example is the polemical woodcut illustrating Luther's *Passional Christi et Antichristi*. Another famous painting, mentioned above, is *Ten Commandments*, which is now exhibited in Luther House. Originally, this work decorated Wittenberg's city hall.

Another of Cranach's well-known works is displayed in Wittenberg's City Church. This painting is known as the "Reformation Altar" and was dedicated by Bugenhagen on April 24, 1547, which was after Luther's death. From a historical point of view, this painting is notable because it was dedicated during the Smalcaldic War, on the same day that Lutheran princes were defeated by the troops of Charles V in the Battle of Mühlberg. The consequences of this battle were soon felt in Wittenberg as well: the elector was captured, Wittenberg lost its residence status, and the city was conquered shortly thereafter.

While painting this altar scene, Cranach was advised by the Wittenberg theologians. The center panel depicts the Lord's Supper. All the disciples are sitting at the table, wearing brightly colored robes, except for Judas Iscariot, who is wearing a yellow robe—an indication of the betrayal yet to come. The servant handing the chalice to Luther is Lucas Cranach the Younger. In this group, Luther is portrayed as Junker Jörg, the way Cranach saw him when the reformer secretly returned from the Wartburg.

In this era, such paintings and illustrations were typically full of meaning because few people could read and write. In that respect they were dependent on pictorial interpretations.

Another of Cranach's famous paintings displayed in Wittenberg's City Church is the epitaph for Paulus Eber,

One of Cranach's most famous paintings illustrates the Ten Commandments.

a professor of theology. The painting depicts a vineyard, the biblical metaphor for the Church, and is based on a statement that Pope Leo X made in his bull threatening excommunication: "The wild boar [Eber is German for "boar"] from the forest will destroy the vineyard, and an extraordinarily wild beast eats it bare."

In this painting, Cranach depicts in a polemical way who is really destroying the vineyard and who is actually taking care of it. Thus, on the left side, the pope, monks, and cardinals are all hard at work, ripping out vines and throwing rocks into the well. On the other side of the painting are the reformers, who are the epitome of devotion to the vines. Luther is seen pulling weeds, Melanchthon is drawing clear water, and Bugenhagen is raking the ground.

After the reformer's wedding, Cranach painted a double portrait of Luther and Katharina, which today exists in several versions. The purpose of the painting is obviously to garner approval of the marriage.

Some years later, a second portrait was made with the couple already looking more mature. Several versions of this portrait have survived as well. The last portrait Cranach made of Luther was in 1539. At age 56, the reformer is portrayed as heavyset and mature, which is probably meant to symbolize Lutheran stability and confidence.

Cranach was and still is known as a successful entrepreneur who owned a number of homes in Wittenberg. He was also one of the richest men in town, second only to Electoral Chancellor Brück. Interestingly, Cranach was even licensed as a pharmacist and had a permit to sell wine in taverns.[55]

Bugenhagen

Because he was from Pomerania in the northeastern part of German lands, Johannes Bugenhagen was also known as "Pommeranus."

After studying Luther's writings, Bugenhagen joined the reformers in 1520. Deciding to study at the Leucorea, he enrolled there in 1521, and with Luther's recommendation, he took the

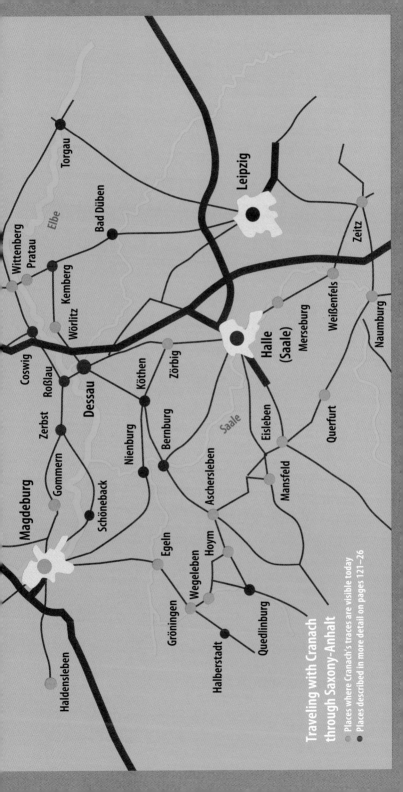

Traveling with Cranach
through Saxony-Anhalt

● Places where Cranach's traces are visible today
● Places described in more detail on pages 121–26

Magdeburg

Haldensleben

Gommern

Zerbst

Schönebeck

Egeln

Gröningen

Wegeleben

Hoym

Halberstadt

Quedlinburg

Roßlau

Coswig

Dessau

Nienburg

Bernburg

Aschersleben

Köthen

Zörbig

Mansfeld

Eisleben

Querfurt

Wörlitz

Kemberg

Pratau

Wittenberg

Bad Düben

Elbe

Saale

Halle
(Saale)

Merseburg

Weißenfels

Leipzig

Zeitz

Naumburg

Torgau

position of Wittenberg pastor and became Luther's pastor and spiritual caretaker. Bugenhagen and Luther were close friends. Bugenhagen married Luther and Katharina, baptized their first child, and gave the sermon at Luther's funeral.

Bugenhagen also assisted in translating the Bible, and his biblical commentaries were influential, especially in Lower Germany. He translated the Bible into Low German.

Wittenberg honors its first Lutheran pastor with a sculpture.

In 1521, Luther hid at the Wartburg (above), while Bugenhagen was beginning his studies in Wittenberg. Little did they know that one day they would become close friends.

The door onto which the Ninety-five Theses were nailed at Wittenberg Castle Church (*Schlosskirche*) symbolizes Luther's struggle against the abuses of his time.

CHAPTER SEVEN
Luther's Struggles against Indulgences

Electronic Indulgences

On September 2, 2004, Christoph Drösser, an editor for the weekly German newspaper *Die Zeit*, wrote the following about indulgences:

> People usually associate indulgences with the lowest point of the Middle Ages—a way of "horse-trading with God" and a practice denounced by Luther. While these days there are no more devious priests who graphically portray the agony of purgatory to the people and then sell a letter of indulgence to let them avoid pain, the Roman Catholic Church in fact continues to hold on to the principle of indulgences. This was last confirmed by Pope Paul VI in the Apostolic Constitution *Indulgentiarum Doctrina* in 1967. Even John Paul II made use of this instrument. Thus, in the Great Jubilee of 2000, believers could ask for a plenary (that is, complete) indulgence of sins.

Indulgences must not be confused with the forgiveness of sins that only God can grant. But, according to the Roman Catholic faith, even sinners who have been forgiven and who have shown active repentance must still pay for their deeds in purgatory. People can avoid this punishment even today by donating money to charitable organizations, by social involvement, by pilgrimages, or by attending special worship services. While indulgences are not "necessary for salvation," as Paul VI said, they can make life after death significantly easier. However, there is no "price list" for sinners.

One good opportunity for gaining indulgences, for instance, would be the pope's *Urbi et Orbi* blessing at Easter. Attendees can receive full indulgence—even if they only attend by means of radio or television.

In Luther's opinion, the sale of indulgences was scandalous because the remission of sins was being mixed together with political and economic goals. He initially denounced this scandalous moneymaking in his lectures and later in his Theses.

In Luther's day, the archbishopric of Mainz was the largest archbishopric in Christianity—and also the seat of the archchancellor of Germany, the head of all the German electors. Because the archbishopric had changed occupants three times between 1504 and 1514, it now had to pay a triple fee to Rome for the appointment of a new archbishop and for the granting of a gallium (the symbol for the rank of archbishop). The price tag: 10,000 ducats or 14,000 guilders.

For this reason, the archbishopric was in extreme debt, which is also why—for the new election—a candidate was sought who would have the necessary finances at his disposal. Enter Albert of Hohenzollern-Brandenburg—who had been the archbishop of Magdeburg since 1513. Even though holding multiple offices was prohibited, Rome still permitted it after a special dispensation was negotiated, plus a payment of 21,000 ducats or 29,000 guilders.

Because Albert did not have this amount at his disposal, the Fugger bank lent it to him. In return, Albert had to permit the selling of the so-called "St. Peter's Indulgence" for the construction of St. Peter's Basilica in Rome. Half of the proceeds would go to Rome—and the other half to the Fuggers to repay the debt. From the outset, there was an obvious intertwining of religious and financial interests regarding the papal bull of indulgence— the so-called *Sacrosancti salvatoris et redemptoris nostri.*

Indulgences were to be sold for a period of eight years in the ecclesiastical provinces of Mainz, Magdeburg, and Brandenburg. With very few exceptions, they would apply to all sins. Consequently, "subcommissioners," preachers of indulgence, and confessors were recruited to execute the indulgence campaign. Therefore, on January 22, 1517, Johann Tetzel—a Dominican monk from Leipzig—was sworn in as general subcommissioner for the sale of indulgences in the ecclesiastical province of Magdeburg.

On April 10 of that same year, Tetzel was in Jüterbog. He was undoubtedly sought out by some people whose confessor was Luther, so that—for the first time—Luther was directly confronted with the effects of "St. Peter's Indulgence."

Initially, Luther tried to clarify the matter in his sermons. While able to appreciate the difficulties with the sacrament of

An indulgence coffer, originally part of a St. Sebastian Altar, 1522.

penance that led to the sale of indulgences, Luther regarded indulgences as the wrong solution to the problem.

Many years later (1541), Luther wrote indignantly about the practice of indulgences:

Meanwhile, I found out what dreadful and abominable articles Tetzel was preaching, and I will mention some of them now: He claimed that he had such grace and power from the pope that even if someone seduced the holy Virgin Mary, the mother of God, or impregnated her, Tetzel could forgive that person, if only he placed the proper amount in the money chest. Similarly, Tetzel claimed that when the red indulgence-cross bearing the papal arms is lifted up in church, it is just as powerful as the cross of Christ. . . . And again, that if anyone puts money in the chest for a soul in purgatory, the soul flies [from purgatory] to heaven as soon as the coin falls and rings at the bottom. Tetzel claimed that the grace from indulgences is the same grace as the grace through which a man is reconciled to God.[56]

The Ninety-five Theses (a selection)

Out of love for the truth and in zeal to ascertain it, the following Theses will be publicly discussed at Wittenberg under the chairmanship of the Reverend Father Martin Luther, Master of Arts and Sacred Theology, and regularly appointed professor there. Therefore, he requests that those who cannot be present to debate orally with us will do so by letter. In the name of our Lord Jesus Christ. Amen.[57]

1. When our Lord and Master Jesus Christ said, "Repent" (Matt. 4:17), He meant that the entire life of a believer should be one of repentance.

5. The pope neither intends nor is able to remit any penalties except those that he has imposed, based on his own decrees or those of the ecclesiastical canons.

21. Therefore, indulgence preachers are in error when they say that a man is free and rid of every punishment by means of papal indulgences.

24. Therefore, unavoidably, the majority of people are completely deceived by those promises boastfully given for the remission of punishments.

27. A man-made teaching is being preached when someone claims that as soon as the money rings in the coffer, a soul flies up (out of purgatory).

28. To be sure, as soon as the money rings in the coffer, profits and greed can increase, but the intercession of the Church is based on God's will alone.

32. Whoever believes that he can be certain of his salvation because of a letter of indulgence will be eternally damned, along with his teachers.

35. It is a non-Christian teaching when someone claims that contrition is not necessary for those who ransom their souls (from purgatory) or for those who purchase letters of absolution.

36. Any Christian who truly repents is entitled to the full remission of punishments and guilt, even without a letter of indulgence.

37. Any true Christian, whether living or dead, partakes in all the blessings of Christ and of the Church that are given to him by God—even without a letter of indulgence.

45. Christians should be taught that whoever sees someone in need, goes past him, and instead pays for indulgences is not buying an indulgence from the pope. Rather, these people will receive the wrath of God.

46. Christians should be taught that whoever does not live in affluence should hold on to the necessities for his household and under no circumstances should squander money on indulgences.

50. Christians should be taught that if the pope knew the coercive methods of the indulgence preachers, he would rather see St. Peter's Basilica reduced to ashes than have it built with the skin, flesh, and bones of his sheep.

51. Christians are to be taught that it would be the pope's wish—as his duty—to give of his own money to very many of those from whom certain hawkers of pardons cajole money, even if the church of St. Peter might have to be sold.

52. It is vain to expect salvation on the basis of a letter of indulgence, even if the (indulgence) commissioner—in fact, even if the pope himself—pledged his own soul for it.

53. Those who arrange for God's Word to be completely silent in surrounding churches in order to preach indulgences are enemies of Christ and the pope.

62. The true treasury of the Church is the holy Gospel of the glory and grace of God.

92. Therefore, away with all those prophets who preach to Christians, "Peace! Peace!" when there is no peace!

93. May it go well with every prophet who preaches to Christians, "Cross! Cross!" when there is no cross!

94. Christians should be encouraged to strive to follow Christ—their Head—through punishments, death, and hell,

95. And they should trust to enter the kingdom of heaven through many tribulations—rather than soothing themselves in false spiritual security.

The 500th Anniversary of the Reformation: October 31, 2017

On October 31, 1517, Luther wrote a submissive and respectful letter to Archbishop Albert, whom we mentioned previously.

Luther was not criticizing the practice of indulgences per se. Rather, he was concerned about misunderstandings arising among the people. As such, buyers of indulgences were being tricked into believing that from that day forward they could be sure of their salvation and that their souls would arrive in heaven as soon as the money was paid, Luther said—referring to Tetzel's ditty: "As soon as a coin in the coffer rings / the soul from purgatory springs." Luther was upset by the claim that people could supposedly be forgiven—even of grave sin—by means of indulgences.

Luther sent a cover letter to the archbishop and included the Ninety-five Theses, which criticized indulgences from a number of different angles. Luther's Theses contain an abundance of arguments and viewpoints, even though he actually intended them to be an academic outline and a basis for discussion.

In his discussion of his Theses, Luther had always—incorrectly—assumed that the pope shared his opinion concerning indulgences. Even in 1541, Luther emphasized that he initially did not intend to oppose indulgences per se—just their misuse.[58] He most certainly did not want to oppose the pope. This is also apparent from his introduction to the Theses (see page 74). But Luther was taken aback by their unintended effect. As soon as the Theses appeared in print, his later observation came true: "It was as though the angels themselves were the messengers and carried it before the eyes of all men."[59]

Luther was mistaken when he assumed that the pope or the ecclesiastical hierarchy would allow his Theses to stand as a starting point for discussion. Case in point, while traveling, Frederick the Wise once had Spalatin read Luther's Theses. Frederick commented, "Mark my words. The pope will not be able to tolerate that."[60]

The Theses were intensely discussed within the Church, and Luther had to write an explanation to them in February and May of 1518.

As the confrontation dragged on, Luther had two tasks before him: first, the difficult and almost hopeless confrontation with the ecclesiastical system and its leadership and, second, building up and implementing his new realization in theory and practice.

The court case against Luther was officially opened in Rome in the summer of 1518. Frederick the Wise, however, managed to arrange that Luther would be summoned not to Rome but to

Augsburg for a hearing before Cardinal Cajetan. That hearing would take place on October 12 and 14 in the Fugger House (*Fuggerhaus*) in that city (see the chapter on Augsburg).

As had been suggested to him, when the hearing began, Luther threw himself humbly on the floor before Cajetan. Yet Cajetan would not swerve from his plan concerning how to conduct the hearing. Cajetan placed three demands on Luther: First, he should return to the fold of the Church. Second, Luther should retract his errors. And third, in the future Luther should refrain from anything and everything that could throw the Church into disarray.

Luther, however, insisted on discussing his Theses against indulgences. Grudgingly, the cardinal gave him his attention, countering Luther with a papal bull from the year 1343 and then with something even weightier—the merit of Christ. Pope Clement VI had asserted in this bull that Christ had earned an excess treasury of good works. For this reason, the Church—according to its own discretion—should surely be allowed to distribute to sinners from that treasury at least for the remission of temporary punishments!

Luther's written reply was rejected by Cajetan. The cardinal asked Luther to recant and threatened him and his supporters with excommunication. In a loud shouting match, Luther refused to recant. Apparently, friends then helped Luther to pass through an unguarded city gate to make a quick escape to Wittenberg, riding the first leg of the journey—to Nuremberg—bareback.

After the Augsburg hearing, a moratorium followed. Luther, however, was eager for a debate. Soon, the Leipzig Debate with Johann Eck—a theology professor from Ingolstadt—would give him just that opportunity.

As Luther wrote to Spalatin on February 7, 1519:

> By the way, our little glory-starved beast, Eck, has published a pamphlet, and according to it, he plans to have a debate with Karlstadt in Leipzig. And since this foolish, jealous man wants to satisfy his long-standing grudge with me, he attacks me and my writings. . . . Consequently, I have published a refutation against him, as you will see

from the enclosed copy. It will perhaps give Eck a reason to finally treat this matter seriously, which up to now he has only treated as a game, and to advise the Roman tyranny to their misfortune.[61]

Many came to hear the debate. Eck, the opponent, was the first to arrive—on June 22—in order to take part in the Feast of Corpus Christi the following day. On June 24, the delegation from Wittenberg made its way through the Leipzig gate in large numbers. In fact, their arrival was so striking that even Eck was given an honor guard of students from Leipzig. During his stay at Leipzig, Luther lived in the house of Melchior Lotter, a printer who lived on Hainstrasse.

After the rules had been negotiated at great length, the actual debate began on June 27. The debate dragged on for more than seventeen days and ended only because Duke George had invited Elector Joachim of Brandenburg as a guest and needed Pleissenburg Castle for his accommodations.

Luther and Karlstadt both tried to defeat Eck in the discussions. Nevertheless, Eck regarded himself as the victor and wrote the pope a letter to that effect in October 1519. In it, he asked the pope to move against Luther for holding to Hussite

Traces of Luther in Leipzig

Luther preached several times in Pleissenburg Castle, Leipzig: on June 29, 1519, on the occasion of his debate with Eck; in the castle's chapel on the eve of Pentecost, on May 24, 1539; in the Church of St. Thomas (*Thomaskirche*) on Pentecost Sunday, May 25, 1539; and in the Church of St. Paul (*Paulinerkirche*), on August 12, 1545.

During his occasional visits to Leipzig, Luther stayed primarily at the home of printer Melchior Lotter (1470–1549), a house that was later called "At the Pear Tree" (*Zum Birnbaum*) and today is the Hôtel de Pologne (Hainstrasse 16/18, indicated by a memorial plaque). He also stayed at the Scherlschen House (which today is located at Klostergasse 3).

The Church of St. Thomas.

heresy. Accordingly, a bull threatening excommunication was posted in Meissen, Merseburg, and Brandenburg in September 1520. It applied not only to Luther but also to Karlstadt, Luther's partner in the debate, and to other followers.

As a result, Luther's books were burned in several cities. Luther reacted to this on December 10, 1520, in Wittenberg—by publicly burning papal books and the canon law,[62] along with the bull threatening excommunication.

On December 10, 1520, Luther wrote to Spalatin:

> Greetings! On December 10, 1520, at nine o'clock in the morning, all these books of the pope will be burned in Wittenberg in front of the eastern gate, near the Church of the Holy Cross: the *Decretum*, the *Decretals*, the *Liber Sextus*, the *Clementines*, the *Extravagantes*, and the newest bull of Leo X . . . as well as several other [writings] that were added by various others so that the Papist arsonists can see that it does not take much to burn books they cannot refute.[63]

Pope Leo X

Leo X (Giovanni de Medici)—pope from March 11, 1513, to December 1, 1521—imposed the bull of excommunication against Luther. Leo had studied theology and canon law in Pisa. At the instigation of his father, he was promoted to cardinal in 1489 and bolstered his family in Florence. After the Medici were driven from Florence—mainly by Girolamo Savanarola, a Dominican—Leo resided in France, Germany, and Flanders, until he returned to Rome after the death of Alexander VI (1503). In 1511, Pope Julius II sent him to Bologna and Romagna. That same year, he was appointed commander-in-chief of the Spanish and papal troops in the war against France.

Leo had little luck in foreign policy. When the emperor was elected in 1519, Leo first supported French King Francis I, then Saxon Elector Frederick the Wise, and finally Spanish King Charles I, who later became head of the Holy Roman Empire until 1556—as Emperor Charles V. In 1521, Leo formed an alliance with Charles V against France.

True to his election promises, Leo summoned a general council, the Fifth Lateran Council (1513–17), which brought no noteworthy results despite beneficial decrees for reform. Above all, the lack of true reform was because both the pope and curia lacked any serious intention for renewal.[64]

The city wall at Worms (*Wormser Stadtmauer*) looms forebodingly against the gloomy sky. In Worms, Luther made his stand against the pope.

CHAPTER EIGHT
Worms—Luther's Confession

On April 16, 1521, Worms—population 7,000—was full of visitors. There was an air of tension in the city because people knew that Luther was going to give a reply before the young emperor at the Imperial Diet, which is what Elector Frederick had accomplished against papal opposition.

Luther's journey to Worms turned into a triumphal procession. His old university in Erfurt had welcomed him enthusiastically, and his monastic church was "standing room only" as he preached there.

Twice, Luther tried to explain his views to the Imperial Diet, but each time he was emphatically asked to recant. As a result, he replied with a long Latin speech, which he concluded with the famous words:

The Worms City Gate (*Wormser Stadttor*).

Since your Imperial Highness and your Majesties desire a plain answer, I will give you such an answer without any horns or teeth. Unless I am convinced by the testimony of Scripture and clear reasoning (for I trust neither the pope nor councils alone, since it is well-known that they have often erred and contradicted themselves), my conscience is bound to the passages in Holy Scripture I have cited. I am held captive by the Word of God. Hence, I cannot and will not retract anything, because it is neither safe nor salutary to go against conscience.

In German, he added:

God help me. Amen.

Thereafter, in the Edict of Worms, Charles V imposed on Luther the status of an outlaw.

Sights in Worms

The Cathedral (*Dom*)

A stone next to the cathedral commemorates the building (which no longer exists) in which the Imperial Diet of Worms was held.

Bishop Burchard had the present cathedral built in the middle of the twelfth century.

The Reformation Monument depicting Luther and other reformers (*Reformationsdenkmal*)

The Luther Monument (*Lutherdenkmal*), depicting the man from Eisleben and other reformers, was unveiled on June 25, 1868. This Luther statue became a role model for depictions of Luther in the nineteenth century and was frequently copied.

A postcard showing the monument around 1900.

Eisenach and Luther's Bible Translation

On his way home, once Luther was in the territory of Electoral Saxony, he was brought to the Wartburg, near Eisenach, in a fake raid carried out by the elector's men. Living there as "Knight George" (*Junker Jörg*), Luther let his hair and beard grow out and was soon no longer recognizable.

Literally a prisoner, Luther was not allowed to leave the vicinity of the castle. Eating food he was not used to and with the lack of activities, he initially did not enjoy his sojourn.

On August 15, 1521, he wrote to Spalatin from the Wartburg:

> Do not let the exile I must bear cause you any worries. . . . Last Monday [August 12] I went hunting for two days to see what this bittersweet pleasure of "heroes" is like. We caught two rabbits and several poor partridges—truly a worthy occupation for men with nothing to do! I theologized even among the snares and dogs. As enjoyable as this endeavor may seem at first glance, however, there was just as much pity and grief that a comparison mixed into it.

> For what does this picture signify other than that the devil hunts animals that are similarly innocent? But instead of snares and dogs, the devil uses godless teachers and, more specifically, bishops and theologians.

> This extremely depressing comparison to simple and believing souls upset me very much. But then an even more dreadful comparison followed.

> Because of my efforts, we kept a little rabbit alive. I wrapped it in the sleeve of my coat and left it alone for a while. Meanwhile, the dogs flushed out the poor rabbit. Biting it through my coat, they first broke its right hind paw and then extinguished its life by a bite to the throat. The pope (and Satan too!) rages in the exact same way: once again, he ruins souls that are already saved and does not care in the least about my efforts.[65]

After his attitude had improved somewhat, Luther began translating the New Testament, placing great emphasis on using language that would be as easy to understand as possible. He consulted Spalatin and Melanchthon as editors during his stays

Hiding out at the Wartburg as "Knight George" (*Junker Jörg*), Luther translated the New Testament into German, thus making it accessible to the German people.

in Wittenberg. Striving for precision and clarity, he even had the elector's treasures brought in for study, in order to better translate the various jewels referred to in Revelation 21:18–21. Melanchthon had the task of converting the value of terms for ancient coins as accurately as possible.

As mentioned previously, the "September Testament" was sold out and out of print within a short period of time.

In his preface to the New Testament, Luther wrote:

So, too, the Gospel of God and the New Testament resonated from the apostles into the whole world as the Good News and as a proclamation of victory by the true David who battled with sin, death, and the devil and overcame them. And in so doing, He redeemed, justified, made alive, and saved all who had been held captive in sin, plagued by death, and overwhelmed by the devil—even though they had not merited their salvation. In that way, He made satisfaction for them and brought them back home to God again. For this reason, they sing, thank, and praise God and are eternally glad, as long as they firmly believe [the Gospel] and remain steadfast in the faith.[66]

Of the four Gospels, Luther had the highest esteem for the Gospel of John. In his preface to the New Testament, Luther wrote: "[The Gospels] are the true and noblest books of the New Testament" (after the 1534 edition of the Bible and the 1539 extra edition of the New Testament, this part is left out). Luther justified his statement:

> Since John writes only a little about the deeds of Christ but quite a lot about His preaching—as opposed to the other three Gospels, which describe many of His deeds but few of His words—John's Gospel is the unmatched, precious, true chief Gospel and by far is preferable to the other three Gospels.[67]

Not only was Luther's translation a theological milestone—it was also a milestone for linguistic history in general. Luther's language was influenced by the dialects of East Middle German and Low German, which were understood by a widespread readership. Because of this, Luther's Bible translation and other works had many readers.

Luther's linguistic contributions impacted the German language in a significant way—and are noticeable even in our day and age. For instance, expressions he coined are still used today,

Today there is a flurry of tourist activity outside the room where Luther once translated the New Testament into German.

such as a Greek phrase, which he rendered as "Wes des Herz voll ist, des geht der Mund über" ("Out of the abundance of the heart the mouth speaks").[68]

Luther's impact and the circulation of his works by the printing press can best be compared to the impact of the Internet in our day.

Luther had the following opinion on this matter:

> I did not use any specific, particular, distinct German dialect. Rather, I used the common speech, so that both upper Germans and lower Germans could understand me. I use the language of Saxon officials, of all the princes and kings in Germany.[69]

Luther and Music

Toward the end of 1523, Luther shared with Spalatin his plan to write German psalms or spiritual songs for the people, so that the Word of God would remain among the people in song as well. He had already composed "From Depths of Woe I Cry to You" and "May God Bestow on Us His Grace." Now Luther was looking for additional competent poets, and he turned to Spalatin—among others—for that purpose:

> I intend to compose rhyming psalms for the people according to the example of the ancient fathers of the Church, that is, spiritual songs by which the Word of God may also remain among the people through song. Hence, we are looking for poets everywhere. Since you are endowed with a richness and elegance in the German language that is refined by extensive use, I am asking you to work on and undertake with us this project of converting a given psalm into a hymn, as you have here an example from me.[70] I would prefer that you avoided new and sophisticated words, so that the simplest and most commonplace words possible are used to match the capabilities of the people. At the same time, the words should be as apt and fitting as possible. In addition, the sense should be clear and as close to the Psalms as possible.[71]

Before writing the chorales mentioned above, Luther had already composed a type of folk song that was circulated as a

flyer. It was based on the following incident: In 1523, two of Luther's brother monks were burned to death at the market-place in Brussels because of their confession of faith. Even in the first lines, Luther conveys his mood: "We lift up a new song to praise the workings of God our Lord, which God has done for His praise and honor . . ."

As Otto Schlisske remarked: "Luther is filled with jubilant joy that what he understood to be true had now manifested itself in others as well—and so powerfully that they were even able to bravely face death for it."[72]

As early as 1523, Luther's first hymns were published individually. One of them was "Dear Christians, One and All, Rejoice"—one of his most impressive musical compositions. A choral hymnal of four books—one for each voice—contained Luther's first collected musical expression for singing in worship services. It was published in Wittenberg in 1524.

It was very important to Luther that young people in particular would learn these new songs and enjoy them. Johann Walter, the cantor of Torgau, is listed as the author of these mostly four-part compositions, while Luther wrote the texts and composed the melodies.

In publishing hymnals, Luther was pursuing various goals. Presumably, evangelism was his primary goal. Also, hymns would spread knowledge of the Bible and the ideas of the Reformation. In addition, rhyming and melody were meant to help people remember Christian content more easily. Finally, singing together would build community. Luther regarded the psychological effects of music as a powerful medicine against evil and as an excellent tool for battling frustration.

Luther composed more than thirty hymns, including hymns for the church year, such as "From Heaven Above to Earth I Come"; hymns based on the catechism, such as "These Are the Holy Ten Commands"; hymns based on the Psalms, such as "A Mighty Fortress Is Our God"; plus songs for use at home and liturgical hymns.[73]

Why Hymns Were So Important

In order to appreciate the importance of hymns, we must consider the level of education in Luther's day. Illiteracy was widespread. In the few cities that existed, only about 20 percent of the population was literate. By comparison, in rural areas only an estimated 2 percent could read and write.

Basically, only clergy and government officials were literate. For this reason, education or instruction could not be imparted by the written word. As such, religious concepts were conveyed though images in churches. Even today, the variety of these images is visible.

Back then, the spoken word had even greater significance. In this regard, the commoners were dependent on "mediators" who could read—especially the village priest. For instance, if a priest did not want to read a pamphlet aloud, the information conveyed in it bypassed the village completely.

On the other hand, if the priest wanted a text read aloud, and also wanted to add his own thoughts that he considered worthy of sharing, then the priest's own ideas would be mixed in with the content of the pamphlet as well.

As early as 989, the Perlach Tower (*Perlachturm*) in Augsburg was built as a watchtower. Its current form was designed by the famous architect Elias Holl (1573–1646).

CHAPTER NINE
Augsburg—The Confession of the Lutheran Church

After Worms, Emperor Charles V continued to try to curtail the Reformation. As such, the Imperial Diet of Augsburg, which convened during the summer of 1530, was meant to "set things right" again.

This Imperial Diet is interesting for several reasons. For one thing, Luther was not the center of attention, despite the fact that the issues negotiated there would be of great significance for the Reformation. This was because the reformer had to remain at a distance because the outlaw status imposed on him at Worms remained in effect. For this reason, he could accompany his princes only as far as the Saxon border.

Monitoring the negotiations at Augsburg from distant Coburg Castle and writing encouraging letters from there, Luther was able to provide only long-distance support to his friend Melanchthon.

At the Diet, Melanchthon presented a summary of the Lutheran faith—the so-called Augsburg Confession (*Confessio Augustana*). Charles V fell asleep during the presentation. The emperor did, however, have a refutation (*confutatio*) read aloud

One of the largest castle compounds in Germany: Coburg Castle (*Veste Coburg*).

that had been drawn up by papal theologians—and with that he considered the problem solved.

Once again, Charles V demanded that the princes follow through with the Edict of Worms, within the time limits defined by him. Because the princes were convinced that the emperor would use force if necessary, they joined forces in a defensive alliance at Smalcald (*Schmalkalden*). In his writing "A Warning to My Dear German People," Luther explained that resisting the Papists—and also the emperor under the given circumstances—was not rebellion, but rather self-defense.

Sights in Augsburg

The Fugger Houses "Am Weinmarkt" (*Fuggerhäuser*)

Jakob Fugger owned several buildings "at the wine market" (*Am Weinmarkt*), now located at Maximilianstrasse 36/38. Luther had his hearing with Cardinal Cajetan in one of them.

Church of St. Anne

This church was part of a former Carmelite monastery (thirteenth century) before it became Lutheran in 1525. Luther stayed in one of the monks' quarters during his hearing with Cardinal Cajetan in 1518.

Luther's Health Problems

Luther commented on his health problems in various letters: On February 27, 1537, he wrote Katie from Tambach:

> I set out from Smalcald yesterday and traveled here in my gracious lord's [that is, the elector's] personal carriage. The reason for this is that the whole time I have been here, I have not been healthy for as much as three days. From last Sunday [February 18] until this evening, not even a drop of water passed from me. I could not rest or sleep. I was unable to hold down any food or drink. In short, I was dead and had already commended you, along with the children, to God and my gracious lord and thought I would never see you again in this mortal life. I felt great pity for you, but I had already resigned myself to the grave. But there was so much fervent prayer to God on my behalf and the tears of many people were so effective that God

Herbs were greatly valued for their medicinal powers. The meadowsweet plant shown here was believed to help against a four-day fever.

opened my bladder this evening and in two hours at least three to four liters passed from me. I feel like I have been born again.[74]

Luther recovered very slowly from the kidney and bladder pains from kidney stones, about which he often complained, but after a while he was able to take up his lecturing and preaching again in early July.

The history of the reformer's illnesses is long, and numerous books have been written on it. In particular, reports from the last years of his life frequently mention his state of health. Several illnesses afflicted him, yet he would not reduce his workload.

Luther responded to the strict dietary restrictions of doctors with skepticism, since he wanted to enjoy the good gifts of God with thanksgiving. Preventative measures were not what he had in mind. Although it is not confirmed that Luther ever made this statement, there are many variations of what Bertolt Brecht[75] quotes Luther as having said:

I will eat what I like and die when God wills it.

Food and Drink in Luther's Day

In Luther's day, menus depended on social status and on the respective food production of the particular time. On feast days, or in autumn after a fruitful summer, or when animals were butchered, there was probably a rich abundance of food, as is often described. In extreme contrast, however, there also were famines after crop failures. Above all, it was the poor peasants and serfs who were affected by crop failures, because they had to offer payment in kind and were thus unable to purchase food for themselves.

Crop failures drove up prices in the regional marketplaces when enough grain seed was unavailable. Because of reduced planting after a crop failure, often another meager harvest would follow. Only when potatoes from South America were introduced would this vicious cycle be broken.

Regarding class distinctions, wild game, poultry, protein-rich meat dishes, wine, and even good wheat bread were reserved for the nobility and rich feudal lords, while simple peasants had to be content with oat bread, rye bread, and beer. Nevertheless, Luther observed that

> Although they do not live as magnificently as kings and princes, the common people still enjoy the best goods, such as peace and tranquility. They also live much more securely and blissfully within their fence than kings and princes do in their castles or fortresses.[76]

Luther also occasionally remarked how dark bread, meat, and beer tasted better to peasants after their hard work than white bread, game, and wine taste to princes. Spices and raw sugar were luxury items in that era. The basic sweetener for common folk was honey.

Since the thirteenth century, writings on proper table manners (*Tischzucht*) informed people about proper behavior at the table. For instance, these rules stipulated that knives should not be scraped off against boots or that people should not blow their noses on tablecloths.

Luther enjoyed "good home-cooking,"[77] along with good drink (wine or beer). He preferred pork to game, which is drier, and would not deprive himself of a short afternoon nap after his midday meal.

He traced illnesses back to the workings of the devil, and thus regarded faith and prayer as the best antidote. However, he was against completely renouncing doctors and medicine because that would be to sinfully tempt God.[78] Nevertheless, Luther did occasionally express that they would need a "new church cemetery" because of all of the doctors' risky treatments. The reformer's frequent attacks of gout are possibly related to his diet.

On August 19, Luther wrote Spalatin about the bubonic plague that was running rampant in 1527:

> The plague has definitely broken out here, though it is relatively merciful. What is astonishing, however, is the fear and flight of the people. Never before have I seen such atrociousness from Satan. . . . Hans Lufft has made a recovery and overcome the plague, and many others would have also recovered if they had accepted medical treatment. But many are so barbarian that they despise medical treatments and die needlessly.

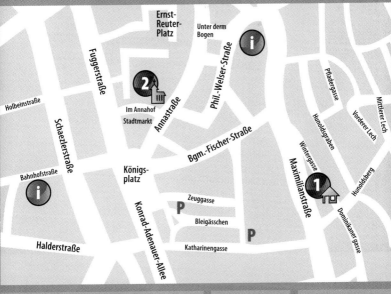

| ❶ | The house on Maximilianstraße 36/38 (*where Luther was questioned by Cajetan*) | ❷ | St. Anne (*St. Anna*) | ⓘ | Information |

In the fifteenth century, Torgau became the permanent residence of the elector. Quite literally, Hartenfels Castle (*Schloss Hartenfels*) is a solid witness of the Reformation era.

CHAPTER TEN
Torgau

Torgau's heyday was in the first half of the sixteenth century. During this period, the Ernestine electors established their residence there and remodeled the existing castle into a Renaissance structure, Hartenfels Castle (*Schloss Hartenfels*).

In the side wing of the castle is the Castle Church (*Schlosskirche*), which was consecrated by Martin Luther on October 5, 1544.[79] During this same period, many impressive homes were constructed for the upper class. Rooms in these homes often have arched ceilings with splendid frescos, some of which have survived.

As the residence of John Frederick the Magnanimous, Torgau became the political center of the Reformation. Luther regularly preached in the castle's chapel and traveled to the city more than forty times. Also, the Augsburg Confession was drawn up there.

A plaque commemorating the Torgau Articles—a document on which the Augsburg Confession was based.

Torgau became the final resting place for Katharina von Bora. Sadly, when Luther died in 1546, her life became a struggle. As if economic insecurity were not bad enough, she had to flee to Magdeburg to avoid being caught up in the Smalcald War. After returning to Torgau for a short while, Katharina then traveled to Braunschweig and then—in July of that same year—returned to Wittenberg.

In 1552, she left the destroyed Black Abbey (*Schwarzes Kloster*) and fled to Torgau to escape the plague. On that journey, she fell and never recovered from the accident. Katharina von Bora died on December 20, 1552, six years after the death of her husband, and was honored with a burial in the City Church of Torgau (*Torgauer Stadtkirche*).

Shortly before his death, on January 25, 1546, Luther wrote his wife:

> To my kind, dear Katie . . . Today at eight we left Halle but could not reach Eisleben. Instead, we got back to Halle at nine, because the "Anabaptist" floods of the river confronted us with waves of water and huge ice floes. Inundating the whole countryside, the waters threatened to "rebaptize" us. Yet we were also unable to return because of the Mulde River near Bitterfeld, and we remained captive here at Halle, surrounded by water—not that we are thirsty to drink it, since we have good beer from Torgau and good Rhine wine. With those drinks, we are refreshing and consoling ourselves in the meantime, in the hope that the Saale River will subside. For since even the locals and ferrymen were fainthearted, we did not want to cross the water and tempt God. For the devil is ill-intentioned toward us and lives in the water.[80]

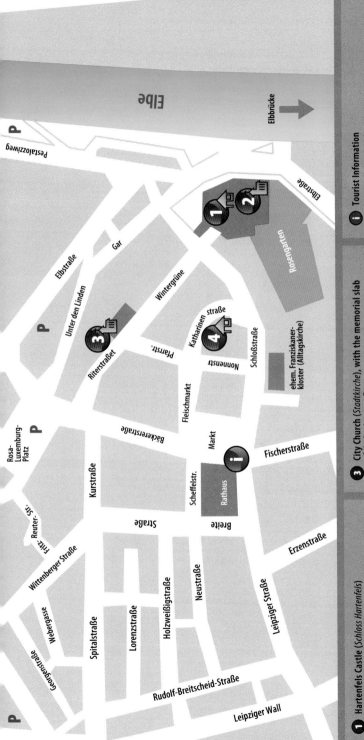

Elbe

→ Elbbrücke

Pestalozziweg

P

Elbstraße

Gar

Unter den Linden

Wintergrüne

P

Riterstraßet

Pfarrstr.

Katharinen- straße

Nonnenstr.

Schloßstraße

Rosengarten

ehem. Franziskaner-
kloster (Alltagskirche)

Fleischmarkt

Bäckerstraße

Kurstraße

Rosa-
Luxemburg-
Platz

P

Reuter-
Str.

Fritz-

Wittenberger Straße

Webergasse

Georgenstraße

Spitalstraße

Lorenzstraße

Holzweißigstraße

Neustraße

Markt

Straße

Scheffelstr.

Breite

Rathaus

Fischerstraße

Erzenstraße

Leipziger Straße

Rudolf-Breitscheid-Straße

Leipziger Wall

① Hartenfels Castle (*Schloss Hartenfels*)
② Castle Church (*Schlosskirche*)
③ City Church (*Stadtkirche*), with the memorial slab of Katharina von Bora
④ Kathrina von Bora´s house (*Katharinas Haus*)

ⓘ Tourist Information

Sights in Torgau

Hartenfels Castle (*Schloss Hartenfels*)

This castle is the greatest completely preserved castle of Germany's early Renaissance period. In the castle's interior is the Stone Spiral (*Wendelstein*), a hanging spiral staircase made of stone almost twenty meters (sixty-five feet) high. Traditionally, bears are still kept in the castle's moat—a practice begun in 1425.[81]

Castle Church (*Schlosskirche*)

The chapel of Hartenfels Castle was the first newly built Protestant church in Germany. In accordance with Luther's instructions, its altar is shaped as a tabletop, which is held by angels. In 1544, the chapel was dedicated by Luther himself.

City Church (*Stadtkirche*), with the memorial slab of Katharina von Bora

The grave of Luther's wife is located in the Church of St. Mary, the oldest church in Torgau (a Romanesque basilica from the year 1119).

Katharina von Bora's House (*Katharinas Haus*)

Katharina von Bora died in this house on Katharinenstrasse 11. Today it is a museum.

Traveling during the Middle Ages

As Luther's letter to Katharina above indicates, traveling was not pleasant during the era of the Reformation. Travelers were directly exposed to the elements and could even be in grave danger—just from bad weather.

Roads were dilapidated, even though the road system was undergoing continual improvement by the end of the Middle Ages. Among the difficulties were detours and waiting periods. Traveling depended on the weather and the political situation. Also, there were only a few bridges at that time.

Trails for pack animals led through the mountains—and such passes were actually relatively numerous. Most of the trails, however, were quite difficult to travel and in winter were almost impassable. In many cases, traveling through the mountains was possible only with the assistance of hired guides.

In good road conditions, one could theoretically cover as many as sixty kilometers (about thirty-seven miles) in one day. On average, however, it was about twenty to forty kilometers (about twelve to twenty-five miles). Someone traveling on foot at a good pace could do six kilometers (just under four miles) an hour or four kilometers (two and a half miles) an hour at a leisurely pace. Traveling more than forty kilometers (about twenty-five miles) each day was a considerable strain for an inexperienced traveler.

Inns were located along the routes at an interval of three to five old German miles. That corresponded to the average day's journey of twenty to forty kilometers (an old German mile is about seven and a half kilometers, less than five miles).

Sea travel was more comfortable and often faster than traveling by land. River voyages were relatively safe, though whirlpools, bridge supports, rocks, and rapids threatened the safety of the travelers. Nights were spent on land.

While traveling, one had to be on guard: holdups and ambushes were common, but simple clothing reduced the risk.

Often, groups of travelers banded together for safety reasons. In many regions, there was also the option of having an official armed escort provided by one of the rulers—for a suitable fee.

In addition, travelers would have to pay customs at customs stations. Pilgrims were generally exempt from these fees, as were merchants, depending on their nationality. Mutual exemption from customs was common for the purpose of opening up markets. As with other German codes of law, the Saxon Code (*Sachsenspiegel*) required travelers to stay on the roads.

Pilgrims could generally travel without money. But other travelers had to pay not only for customs, escort fees, accommodations, and provisions but also for coachmen, a ship captain, guides, or navigators, as applicable. In particular, those traveling with horses had to expect high costs, since food, stable rental, transportation (for example, over rivers), and care consumed large sums of money.

Holding the Bible in his left hand and the bull of excommunication in his right hand, the reformer, as depicted in Eisleben's Luther Monument (*Lutherdenkmal*) (1883).

CHAPTER ELEVEN
Eisleben—Luther's Last Journey

Luther was on good terms with the counts of Mansfeld. At one point, the counts had a falling out with each other over a mining-related issue. Several attempts to reconcile the two parties failed; therefore, Luther was asked to mediate. The meeting was scheduled to take place in Eisleben.

The journey was arduous, and Katharina was greatly concerned about her husband.

The negotiations lasted until February 17. On that last day, Luther could no longer participate because of his weakness. He had dinner with his companions, went to his room, and said his evening prayers at eight o'clock. Shortly thereafter, he was plagued by pains, particularly chest pains, which probably were caused by *angina pectoris*. Aurifaber, one of his companions, went to the counts to obtain some medication made from the shavings of the horn of a unicorn. Afterward, Luther was able to sleep again, but he woke up at one o'clock in the morning with more pain, expecting he might well die in the city of his birth. He confidently prayed Psalm 68:20: "Our God is a God of salvation, and to GOD, the Lord, belong deliverances from death."

One of Luther's last prayers has been handed down with only a few variations. It is a prayer revealing his life with God, in light of the Gospel that he discovered.

In 1566, his friend and first biographer, Johann Matthesius, described the end of Luther's life and his last prayer:

> "O my heavenly Father, God and Father of our Lord Jesus Christ, God of all comfort, I thank You that You have revealed to me Your dear Son, Jesus Christ, in whom I believe, whom I have preached and confessed, whom I have loved and praised, whom the wretched pope and all godless dishonor, persecute, and blaspheme.

> "I ask You, my Lord Jesus: let my soul be commended into Your hands. O heavenly Father, even though I am leaving

this body and am being torn away from this life, I still know for certain that I will remain by You forever and that no one can tear me out of Your hands. . . . [The Bible verses of John 3:16 and Psalm 68:20 follow in Latin.]"

When all sorts of medicine were pushed on him, he said once more, "I am going away," and spoke, "Into Your hands I commit my spirit; You have redeemed me, O Lord, faithful God," three times, one very quickly following the other. Then he became quiet.

Some of his friends shook, rubbed, cooled, and called to him, but he shut his eyes. Dr. Jonas and M. Coelius called out loudly to him: "Dear father, do you wish to die, trusting fully in Christ and in the doctrine you steadfastly preached [that is, without recanting or changing anything]?" [Then] he said, "Yes," so that it could be clearly heard and understood. With that, he fell asleep in the name of Jesus Christ without any bodily agony, quietly and in great peace on February 18 at three in the morning.[82]

For Elector John Frederick, the death of his protégé was a great loss. He arranged for the reformer's body to be returned to Wittenberg and buried in the Castle Church (*Schlosskirche*).

Luther was wrapped in a white gown and transported in a pewter casket to the nearby Church of St. Andrew

The grave of Martin Luther.

The inscription on Luther's gravestone.

(*St.-Andreaskirche*). On February 19, Justus Jonas preached Luther's funeral sermon. The following day, Michael Coelius preached a second funeral sermon. The body was carried from the city toward Halle, where it was kept overnight in the sacristy of the Church of St. Mary (*St.-Marienkirche*). The next day, the procession reached Bitterfeld in Electoral Saxony.

On February 22, the burial took place in Wittenberg, with Bugenhagen preaching the sermon and Melanchthon giving a memorial speech by the casket. The location of the grave was chosen with great care—under the pulpit—because this was Luther's most important place of work.

In his memorial speech, Melanchthon said:

> Who of those who knew him did not know what magnificent humanity he possessed, how friendly he was in his personal exchanges with others, how rarely he was quarrelsome or cantankerous! And yet everything was related to the zeal that is fitting for such a man. . . . Hence, it is clear that his harshness elsewhere flowed out of zeal for the truth, not out of quarrelsomeness or bitterness. Of that, we and many who are not present are all witnesses.[83]

Sights in Eisleben

Luther's Birth House
(*Luthers Geburtshaus*)

Luther's Birth House (see picture on page 2) was built in the middle of the fifteenth century and was located in town. Martin Luther was born there November 10, 1493. As early as 1693, the city renovated the home as a memorial site for Luther and the Reformation. Thus it is one of the oldest museums in the German-speaking world. Luther School (*Lutherschule*) was built on the neighboring property in 1817 for the 300th anniversary of the Reformation.

Luther Monument
(*Lutherdenkmal*)

The Luther Monument located at the marketplace was constructed by Rudolf Siemering in 1883.

Church of St. Andrew
(*St. Andreas*)

Martin Luther gave his last sermon in this church. Most of this Late Gothic hall church was constructed in the fifteenth century. The Baroque domes of the "watchman towers" (*Hausmannstürme*) date from the year 1601. Virtually no changes have been made to the pulpit since Luther's day. In the aisles are tombs of the Mansfeld counts. The busts of the reformers Martin Luther and Philipp Melanchthon were made by Johann Gottfried Schadow.

Luther's Death House
(*Luthers Sterbehaus*)

Luther spoke his last words in this patrician's house, built around 1500 in the Late Gothic style.

Church of Saints Peter and Paul (*St. Petri-Pauli*)

This hall church with three naves—first documented in 1333—is where Martin Luther was baptized.

Church of St. Anne (*St.-Annen-Kirche*)

The miners' Church of St. Anne dates from the year 1514, when the cornerstone was laid. The Augustinian Hermit Monastery (founded in 1515) was directly affiliated with the church. Serving as district vicar of the Augustinian Order, Luther visited this first Lutheran church in the area of Mansfeld several times.

The "Eisleben Stone Picture Bible" (*Eisleber Steinbilderbibel*), fashioned by Hans Thon Uttendrup from Münster in 1585, is noteworthy. It consists of twenty-nine sandstone slabs in relief and depicts important scenes from the Old Testament.

Eisleben is well-known for its charming and relaxing atmosphere.

Luther's solitary struggle against the power of Rome is symbolized by enormous St. Peter's Square.

CHAPTER TWELVE

Luther's Opponents

In the last years of his life, Luther was increasingly concerned about the future of his country and of the Lutheran Church—particularly in light of such grievances as miserliness, usury, immorality, sectarianism, the hostility of Rome against Lutheranism, and, last but not least, even conversions to Judaism.[84]

Because many of these things are "nonissues" these days, Luther's displeasure over them is often no longer understood today. Rather, in contrast to Melanchthon's kind assessment offered above, many people today feel that Luther's railing against these issues must have been triggered by a general feeling of malaise or grumpiness caused by his declining health. If that is true, however, it is unclear why his final letters to Katharina are rather humorous and cheerful and scarcely reveal a trace of grumpiness.

Luther and the Jews

Luther's attitude toward the Jews changed over the years. In 1523, he published the writing "That Jesus Christ Was Born a Jew," trying to evangelize them. At this point in his ministry, he was against anyone who would discriminate against Jews.

Yet by the end of his life, Luther was disappointed that his attempts at attracting Jews for the Gospel were unsuccessful, and thus he wrote books against them.[85] Case in point, he sarcastically describes the sculpture on the City Church (*Stadtkirche*) at Wittenberg:

> Here in Wittenberg there is a pig carved in stone on our parish church. Under it are young piglets and Jews who are suckling. Behind the pig stands a rabbi, who is lifting up the pig's right leg and pulling its rear[86] over himself with his left hand. Stooping over, he is diligently looking at the pig from under its rear, peering into the Talmud, as though

The "Jewish Sow" on the City Church (*Stadtkirche*) of Wittenberg.

intending to read and discover some subtle and special detail.[87]

His writing "On the Jews and Their Lies"[88] (1543) calls for synagogues to be burned down and for the Jews who do not want to work to be banished from the cities—following the example of France, Spain, and Bohemia.[89]

While Bertolt Brecht considers critique of Luther on these issues to be legitimate, he does arrive at the fair conclusion that "Luther's hostility toward the Jews should not be interpreted as psychological or as pathologically hate-filled. It is not political, nor an extension of governmental anti-Judaism. Rather, Luther's . . . conflict with the Jews was essentially religious and theological."[90] Centuries later, the National Socialists would use Luther's theologically motivated hostility toward Jews for their racially motivated anti-Semitism.

The following 1543 mandate on Jews in Electoral Saxony explicitly ascribes the ethical faults of Jews to their "bloodline" and in that respect cannot be credited to Luther. The mandate demands:

> First, their synagogues or schools should be set on fire, and whatever does not burn up should be piled up and covered so that no one may see a stone or ashes from it forever, and such should be done to the glory of our Lord and Christianity. In this way, God will see that we are Christians and have not knowingly endured or condoned such public lies, curses, and blasphemies of His Son and our Christ. . . .
>
> Moses writes that when a city practices idolatry, it should be completely destroyed with fire, and nothing should be left remaining of it. If he were alive today, he would be the first to set the Jewish schools and houses on fire. . . .
>
> As they have clearly persecuted us Christians around the world from the very beginning, and still would gladly do so if they were able, Jews have often also tried to and were forcefully struck on the snout for it. From childhood on, they have imbibed such bitter hatred toward the *Goiim* [Gentiles] from their parents and rabbis, and they continuously imbibe hate into themselves so that it runs through the blood and flesh, through the marrow and bones, and has become their nature and way of life—through and through. . . .
>
> Therefore, dear Christian, know this and do not doubt that—with the exception of the devil—you have no more bitter, venomous, and fierce enemy than a true Jew who earnestly intends to be a Jew. There may well be those among them who believe what the cattle and geese believe; nevertheless, the bloodline adheres to them all. Hence, they are often blamed in historical accounts for poisoning wells and stealing and impaling children. . . .

Luther and the Turks

In the sixteenth century, the Turks posed a tremendous challenge to the Christian West, since this Islamic superpower had control over the Near East, North Africa, and the Balkans. In 1526, they defeated the Hungarian army, and in 1529, they stood at the gates of Vienna, where they were, however, fought off.

This issue was very much on Luther's mind, and he even referred to the Turkish war in his Thesis Five (of the Ninety-five Theses). In his writing "On War Against the Turk," he rejected the latter's right to attack other countries. He was able to refer to the Qur'an in his polemics, since he was familiar with the Latin version of it.

Luther and the Pope

Through his conflict with the pope, Luther called the central figure of the Catholic Church into question and in so doing brought about the break. For this reason, Luther achieved global significance.

He wrote several books against the papacy. One of the most well-known is "Christ and Antichrist," in which Luther comments crassly on ten equally crass caricatures of the pope. On the occasion of the council that convened in Trent in March 1545, a writing of Luther's was published: "Against the Roman Papacy, an Institution of the Devil." In it, he describes the pope as the "antichrist and werewolf, as an enemy of God, an enemy of Christ, and an enemy of all Christians and the whole world," and he warns that anyone who follows the pope must know "that he is obedient to the devil in opposition to God."

Opponents in "Luther's Own Camp"

Thomas Münzer

Initially, Thomas Münzer was a staunch admirer of Luther, being called as a pastor in Zwickau on the reformer's recommendation. However, Münzer was soon dismissed because of his radical sentiments. For more than a year he was unable to find a new parish until he was called to the New City Church (*Neustadtkirche*) in Allstedt in 1523. There he gained many followers.

Again and again, conflicts arose between Münzer and the theologians in Wittenberg. Münzer founded a secret society in 1523, with the goal "of supporting the Gospel, to no longer give any payments to monks and nuns, and to work toward their demise and expulsion."

Luther was greatly troubled by this development and feared violent actions and rebellion would take place. Meanwhile, in a sermon to the princes, Münzer explained his theological views and demonstrated several areas in which he disagreed with Luther. For example, he rejected Luther's doctrine of the two kingdoms (which makes a distinction between the worldly and spiritual kingdoms) and approved of violent actions such as iconoclasm. Münzer attacked Luther as a conformist hypocrite, while Luther viewed Münzer as a false prophet because he explicitly relied on direct revelation from God and downplayed the Bible.[91]

This conflict escalated in the so-called Peasants' War. While Luther viewed peasants who rebelled against and broke the trust of their rulers as murderers and robbers, Münzer supported such peasants and even instigated a rebellion in Thuringia.

During this period, Luther wrote "Against the Rioting Peasants," which was also a special publication entitled "Against the Robbing and Murdering Hordes of Peasants." Münzer would not budge from his views and refused to negotiate with Luther.

Before the Battle of Frankenhausen, Münzer wrote to Count Ernst of Mansfeld:

> You wretched, miserable sack of maggots! Who made you the prince of the people? . . . If you will not humble yourself before the lowly, an eternal disgrace before all Christianity will fall on your neck! You will become the devil's martyr.[92]

Luther was proved right about Münzer, however. After the devastating defeat of the peasants in the Battle of Frankenhausen, the rebel leader hid in bed, pretended to be sick, and denied his identity and any association with the Peasants' War. Found guilty when a incriminating letter was discovered in his pocket,[93] Münzer was executed in Mühlhausen on May 27, 1525.[94]

Luther and Erasmus of Rotterdam

Luther had fundamental theological debates with Erasmus of Rotterdam, a Dutch theologian and humanist. In 1524, the Dutchman began the battle in his *Discourse on the Freedom of the Will (De libero arbitrio diatribe)*, which attacked Luther's *Assertion*[95] that man has no freedom of the will in theological matters—a teaching condemned by Pope Leo.

Erasmus writes:

> Soon afterward, however, it was being forcefully promoted by Martin Luther, whose Assertion on free will is available. Although various parties responded to him, I, too, will respond—having been encouraged to do so by good friends. . . . I am sure that Luther himself would not be offended if someone took a different opinion than his.[96]

Replying in *On the Bondage of the Will*, Luther at first shows respect for Erasmus's gentle style and eloquence.[97] Near the end of his writing, Luther even praises Erasmus:

> Again I applaud and commend you also for this especially: you alone—unlike all the others—have tackled the real issue, the very heart of the matter. . . . You and you alone have recognized the point on which everything hinges, and you have gone straight for the throat.[98]

But only ten lines later, Luther lets Erasmus know:

> God has not yet willed nor granted that you would be any match in this issue of ours.

Luther asserts that God's commands cannot be kept by mere human strength. Rather, the Commandments are meant to lead to the awareness of sin, in accordance with Romans 3:20. Luther concludes with a confession:

> Even if it were somehow possible, I would still not desire free will to be given to me. For even if I lived and could work at it forever, my conscience would never be certain or secure of how much it must do for it to be enough for God. . . . But now, since God has taken my salvation from my will and has placed it on His will, and has promised to keep me by His grace and mercy, I am secure and certain that He is faithful and will not lie to me, also that He is so powerful and strong that no devil and no adversity will be able to overpower Him or to snatch me away from Him.[99]

Luther gave the humanist credit for his skepticism of the Catholic Church, but he criticized both Erasmus's acceptance of Rome's unbiblical rites and his understanding of free will as being "popish." On top of that, Luther considered Erasmus's language to be unclear, indecisive—and even jeopardizing people's faith.[100]

For his part, Erasmus wrote the following about Luther in a letter to Ulrich Zwingli in 1523, regarding the deaths of three Lutheran martyrs:

> I do not know whether I should mourn their death. Of course they went to their deaths with the greatest and most incredible dedication—not for the articles [of faith] but for the nonsensical assertions of Luther, for which I would not die because I am not convinced by them. I know that it is glorious to die for Christ. There is never a lack of affliction for the godly, but even the godless are afflicted, and [the devil] is full of trickery and disguises himself as an angel of light again and again [2 Corinthians 11:14]. Likewise, rare is the gift of distinguishing between spirits [1 Corinthians 12:10]. Luther says some puzzling things that are blatantly absurd: "All the works of saints are sins in need of God's pardoning mercy." Or: "Free will is only an empty name." Or: "A man is justified through faith alone, without works being added to it." I fail to see the advantage of fighting for this, as Luther wants to do.[101]

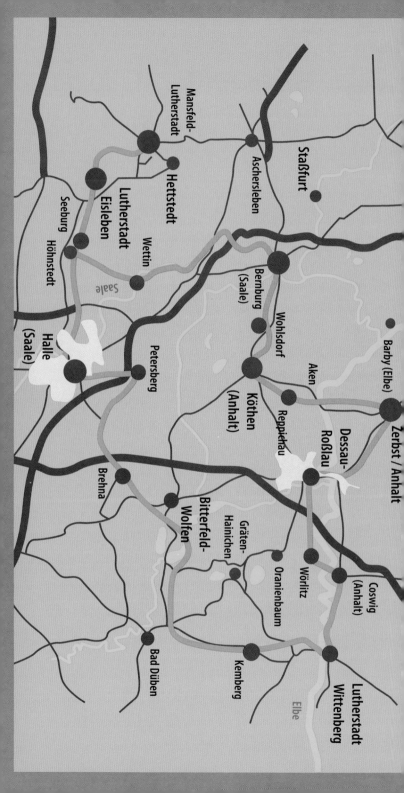

Appendix

[Note: Telephone numbers are listed as they would be dialed within Germany. To telephone Germany from the United States, remove the leading 0 from the phone number and dial 011 + 49 before the number. The Internet addresses are to German sites. Many search engines provide links to translate Web pages. One can also look for a British flag or even the word "English" on some sites. Clicking it will connect to an English-language page.]

The Luther Tour

An expansive Luther Tour (*Lutherweg*) has been created for the 500th anniversary of the Reformation in the year 2017. At present, thirty-six stops are planned. In addition to the Luther sights in Eisleben and Wittenberg already mentioned, it includes the following:

In Coswig, the Church of St. Nicholas (*St.-Nicolai-Kirche*). A previous church was built here in 1150. Sights include a Gothic choir as well as paintings by Cranach the Younger.
　　Address: Schlossstrasse 58, 06869 Coswig
　　Tel.: 03 49 03/6 29 38; www.kirche-coswig.de

In Wörlitz, the originally Romanesque Church of St. Peter (*St.-Petri-Kirche*) was consecrated in 1201. Under Prince Franz of Anhalt-Dessau, it was renovated in neo-Gothic style. The platform of the 66-meter (216-foot) high steeple offers a delightful view of the nearby park. Luther preached here before the Ascanian princes in November 1532. The steeple is also used as a Bible museum.
　　Address: Kirchgasse 34, 06786 Wörlitz
　　Tel.: 03 49 05/2 05 08
　　www.gartenreichkirchen.de **OR** www.bibelturm.de

Dessau offers the following sights: The Wörlitz Garden Realm (*Wörlitzer Gartenreich*), the Johannbau Palace, the Church of St. John (*St.-Johannis-Kirche)*, and the Georgium Palace.

The Wörlitz Garden Realm, a UNESCO World Heritage Site, was created by Franz of Anhalt-Dessau (1740–1817) and is an excellent example of an Enlightenment Age garden.
Address: Schloss Grosskühnau, 06846 Dessau-Rosslau
Tel.: 03 40/64 61 50; www.gartenreich.com

The Johannbau Palace is a former royal residence with an exhibition of the culture and history of Anhalt.
Address: Schlossplatz 3a, 06844 Dessau
Tel.: 03 40/2 20 96 12; www.stadtgeschichte.dessau.de

The Church of St. John (*St.-Johannis-Kirche*) is centrally located in Dessau. Displayed inside are three paintings by Cranach.
Address: Johannisstrasse 11, 06844 Dessau
Tel.: 03 40/21 49 75

The Georgium Palace houses the Anhalt Art Museum (*Gemäldegalerie*). Works of Dürer and Cranach are kept there.
Address: Puschkinallee 100, 06846 Dessau
Tel.: 03 40/66 12 60 00; www.georgium.de

In Rosslau, the Church of St. Mary (*St.-Marien-Kirche*) is part of the Luther Tour. Even in Luther's day, a church was located there, and the reformer spent many a night in the vicinity. The existing church was built in 1854 and houses a 1,000-year-old baptismal bell, as well as several pictures from the workshop of Lucas Cranach.
Address: Grosse Markstrasse 9, 06862 Rosslau
www.kirche-rosslau.de

In Zerbst, you can visit the Francisceum—a German secondary school (*gymnasium*), which owes its existence to Martin Luther. He preached here on several occasions. Today, the city museum (*Stadtmuseum*) is located here. It features a Bible from the workshop of Cranach.

Address: Weinberg 1, 39261 Zerbst/Anhalt
Tel.: 0 39 23/42 28; www.stadt-zerbst.de
email: museum.zerbst@t-online.de

Holy Trinity Church (*St.-Trinitatis-Kirche*), a Baroque-era building, and the Gothic-era Church of St. Nicholas (*St.-Nicolai-Kirche*) are located close to each other. Formerly the largest church in Anhalt, the Church of St. Nicholas was heavily damaged in World War II. The nave has no roof, but the facade of the two steeples has been preserved. Holy Trinity Church was built by 1696 under Prince Carl Wilhelm, a Lutheran.

Address: Rennstrasse 7, 39261 Zerbst
Tel.: 0 39 23/32 91; www.sanktnicolai-zerbst.de

In Reppichau, the Sachsenspiegel Museum presents one of the first German law books, the Saxon Code (*Sachsenspiegel*). Its author was Eike von Repgow, whose name probably stems from the name of the village.

Address: Akener Strasse 3a, 06386 Reppichau
Tel.: 03 49 09/7 07 00; www.reppichau.de

In Köthen, the Church of St. James (*St.-Jakobs-Kirche*) and the Bach Memorial (*Bachgedenkstätte*) are part of the Luther Tour. This Late Gothic church dates to 1518. It became Lutheran because of Prince Wolfgang of Anhalt. In the crypt are tombs from various family lines of princes. One of them is the tomb of Prince Leopold (1694–1728), who was often called "Bach's Prince."

Address: Hallesche Strasse 15a, 06366 Köthen
Tel.: 0 34 96/21 41 57; www.koethen-anhalt.de

The Bach Memorial is located in the Köthen Palace (*Schloss Köthen*). The world-famous composer and musician served as court music director for Prince Leopold of Anhalt-Köthen. In the Ludwigsbau is an exhibition with information on Bach's work.

Address: Schlossplatz 4, 06366 Köthen

Tel.: 0 34 96/21 25 46; www.kulturstaetten-koethen.de

Wohlsdorf Church (*Wohlsdorfer Kirche*), a Romanesque structure, features at its entrance a cross of the Order of the Knights Templar. This church was reformed in 1518 and is presently not in use, though there are plans to revive it again.

Address: Dorfstrasse, 06408 Wohlsdorf

Tel.: 03 47 22/3 10 57

In Bernburg, the former royal castle (*Schloss Bernburg*) of the princes and, later, of the dukes of Anhalt Bernburg, is located on the eastern bank of the Saale River. It was converted into a royal castle in the sixteenth century. In the castle's museum (*Schloss-museum*), sights include valuable editions of Luther's works as well as original reliefs of Lutheran princes.

Address: Schlossstrasse 24, 06406 Bernburg

Tel.: 0 34 71/62 50 07; www.museumschlossbernburg.de

The Church of St. Mary (*St.-Marienkirche*), a Gothic edifice, was first documented in 1228. Prince Wolfgang introduced the Reformation here in 1526.

Address: Breite Strasse 81, 06406 Bernburg

Tel.: 0 34 71/35 36 13; www.bernburger-marienkirche.de

In Wettin, the City Church of St. Nicholas (*St. Nikolai*) dates from the thirteenth century and was modified in the sixteenth century according to Lutheran standards.

Address: Könnersche Strasse 3, 06198 Wettin

Tel.: 03 46 07/2 04 34

Seeburg Castle (*Schloss Seeburg*) dates to the eleventh century. It belonged to the counts of Mansfeld. Luther wrote his sermon for princes (*Fürstenpredigt*) during a stay here.

Address: Schlossstrasse 18, 06317 Seeburg

Tel.: 03 47 74/7 08 68; www.seeburg-schloss.de

In Halle, we recommend visiting the State Museum of Prehistory (*Landesmuseum für Vorgeschichte*), the Church of Our Lady (*Marktkirche Unserer lieben Frauen*), and the Francke Institutions (*Franckesche Stiftungen*).

The State Museum of Prehistory calls the Nebra Sky Disk its own. From October 31, 2008, to October 31, 2009, a special exhibition entitled "Luther's Lost and Found" (*Fundsache Luther*) was held. This special exhibition presented new archaeological finds from Wittenberg and Mansfeld.

Address: Richard-Wagner-Strasse 9, 06114 Halle/Saale

Tel.: 03 45/5 24 73 61; www.fundsache-luther.de

The Church of Our Lady is known for its death mask of Martin Luther and an altar by Cranach. The church's two pairs of steeples are part of the city's silhouette and have been captured by many artists, including Lyonel Feininger. Cardinal Albert, Luther's opponent, had this new large church built from two medieval churches. On Good Friday 1541, Luther's close friend, Justus Jonas, held the first Lutheran worship service there.

Address: An der Marienkirche 2, 06108 Halle/Saale

Tel.: 03 45/5 17 08 94; www.marktkirche-halle.de

The Francke Institutions, founded at Halle in 1698 by theologian and educator August Hermann Francke, house a multitude of cultural, academic, pedagogical, and social facilities. Noteworthy are its coulisse library, the longest half-timbered structure in Europe, and an original museum of art and natural history (*Kunst- und Naturalienkammer*).

Address: Franckeplatz 1, Haus 37, 06110 Halle/Saale

Tel.: 03 45/2 12 74 50; www.francke-halle.de

The monastery on the Petersberg is another sight worth visiting. This Romanesque monastic church dates from the twelfth century and forms the middle section of the compound. The church is the burial place of the princes of the Wettin family line. Surrounded by a Romanesque cloister garden, the ruins of the cloister are also open to the public. The Evangelical Community of the Christ-Brotherhood invites the public to visit and stay for a retreat.

> Address: Bergweg 11, 06193 Petersberg
> Tel.: 0 46 06/2 04 09; www.christusbruderschaft.de

In Brehna, the Church of St. James (*St.-Jakobs-Kirche*) was once part of a Romanesque cloister complex. Katharina von Bora, who later became the wife of Martin Luther, was a pupil here. Today, the church is a roadside chapel (*Autobahnkirche*) that invites travelers to stay for a while.

> Address: Bahnhofstrasse 8, 06796 Brehna
> Tel.: 03 49 54/4 82 09; www.autobahnkirche-brehna.de

Kemberg near Wittenberg was often the destination of Luther's ecclesiastical visitations. In 1521, Luther's friend Provost Bernhardi from Kemberg was the first clergyman to marry, thus establishing the first Lutheran parsonage. Part of a Cranach altar is located in the church.

> Address: Kreuzstrasse 8, 06901 Kemberg
> Tel.: 03 49 21/2 04 07; email: Lampadius@web.de

In Gräfenhainichen, visit the Paul Gerhardt Chapel (*Paul-Gerhardt-Kappelle*). The greatest hymn poet of the Lutheran church was born in this city. The Classicism-era chapel houses a permanent exhibition, as well as a library.

> Address: Breitscheidstrasse 7, 06773 Gräfenhainichen
> Tel.: 03 49 53/3 57 57; www.graefenhainichen.de

General information about the Luther Tour:
> www.lutherweg.de **AND** www.tourismusregion-wittenberg.de

Details and Contact Information

[Note: Telephone numbers are listed as they would be dialed within Germany. To telephone Germany from the United States, remove the leading 0 from the phone number and dial 011 + 49 before the number. The Internet addresses are to German sites. Many search engines provide links to translate Web pages. One can also look for a British flag or even the word "English" on some sites. Clicking it will connect to an English-language page.]

Chapter 1: The Roots

For Eisleben, see chapter 11.

1.1 Möhra

General Information
Local and Tourist Association of Möhra
(*Heimat- und Wanderverein Möhra e.V*)
G. Erbe
Tel.: 0 36 95/8 43 80

1.2 Mansfeld

General Information
Mansfeld City Information (*Stadtinformation Mansfeld*)
Junghuhnstrasse 2
06343 Mansfeld
Tel.: 03 47 82/9 03 42
Fax: 03 47 82/9 03 42 44
E-mail: stadtinfo@mansfeld.eu
See also www.eisleben-tourist.de (Luther's Traces in Mansfeld)
Business Hours:
Monday–Friday, 9 a.m.–12 p.m. and 1:30–3:30 p.m.

The House of Luther's Parents (*Luthers Elternhaus*)
Spangenbergstrasse 2

Church of St. George (*St. Georg*)
Lutherstrasse

Mansfeld Castle (*Schloss Mansfeld*)
Schloss 1
06343 Mansfeld-Lutherstadt
Tel.: 03 47 82/2 02 01

1.3 Magdeburg

General Information
Magdeburg Tourism Association
(*Magdeburg Tourismus GmbH*)
Domplatz 1b
39104 Magdeburg
Tel.: 03 91/1 94 33
Fax: 03 91/83 80-410
E-mail: info@magdeburg-tourist.de
www.magdeburg-tourist.de
Business Hours:
November–March: Monday–Friday, 10 a.m.–6 p.m. and
Saturday, 10 a.m.–3 p.m.
April to October: Monday–Friday, 10 a.m.–6:30 p.m. and
Saturday, 10 a.m.–4 p.m.

Chapter 2: Eisenach and Wartburg Castle

General Information
Eisenach Tourism Association
(*Tourismus Eisenach GmbH*)
Markt 9
D-99817 Eisenach
Tel.: 0 36 91/7 92 30
Fax: 0 36 91/79 23 20
E-mail: info@eisenach.info
www.eisenach-tourist.de

Wartburg
The Wartburg Foundation (*Wartburg-Stiftung*)
Auf der Wartburg
D-99817 Eisenach
Tel.: 0 36 91/25 00
Fax: 0 36 91/20 33 42
E-mail: info@wartburg-eisenach.de
www.wartburg-eisenach.de
Business Hours:
Open year-round: March–October: 8:30 a.m.–5 p.m.
     November–February, 9 a.m.–3:30 p.m.

Luther House (*Lutherhaus***)**
Lutherhaus Eisenach
Lutherplatz 8
D-99817 Eisenach
Tel.: 0 36 91/2 98 30
Fax: 0 36 91/29 83 31
E-mail: lutherhaus@t-online.de
www.lutherhaus-eisenach.de

Concerts in the main hall of the Wartburg take place from May to October.
Organ concerts in the chapel of the Wartburg are held during Thuringia's "Bach Weeks" around Easter.

Chapter 3: Erfurt
General Information
The Tourism Society of Erfurt
(*Tourismus Gesellschaft Erfurt mbH*)
Benediktsplatz 1
D-99084 Erfurt
Tel.: 03 61/66 40-0
Fax: 03 61/66 40-2 90
E-mail: service@erfurt-tourist-info.de
www.erfurt-tourist-info.de

Evangelical Augustinian Convent at Erfurt
(*Evangelisches Augustinerkloster zu Erfurt*)
Augustinerstrasse 10
99084 Erfurt
Tel.: 03 61/57 66 00
Fax: 03 61/5 76 60 99
E-mail: AK-Erfurt@augustinerkloster.de
www.augustinerkloster.de
Business Hours:
April–October: Monday–Saturday (tours hourly), 10 a.m.–5 p.m.
    Sunday, 11 a.m.–3 p.m.
November–March: Monday–Saturday (tours hourly): 10 a.m.–4 p.m.
    Sunday, 11 a.m.–3 p.m.
Invitation for Prayer: In the Augustinian convent, the sisters of
    the Community of Castell (*Communität Casteller Ring*) have
    been working and praying as a religious order according to
    the Rule of St. Benedict of Nursia since 1996.
Prayer times in the church (daily except for Tuesdays): 7 a.m.,
    12 p.m., 6 p.m., and 7:30 p.m. (except for Saturdays)

Chapter 5: Wittenberg

General Information
Wittenberg Information (*Wittenberg-Information*)
Schlossplatz 2
D-06886 Lutherstadt Wittenberg
Tel.: 0 34 91/49 86 10
Fax: 0 34 91/49 86 11
E-mail: wb_info@wittenberg.de
www.wittenberg.de

Luther House (*Lutherhaus*)
The Society of Luther Memorials in Saxony-Anhalt (*Stiftung
    Luthergedenkstätten in Sachsen-Anhalt*)
Collegienstrasse 54
06886 Lutherstadt Wittenberg
Tel.: 0 34 91/42 03-0
Fax: 0 34 91/42 03-2 70

Melanchthon House (*Melanchthonhaus*)
(You may also contact the Society of Luther Memorials)
Collegienstrasse 60
Tel.: 0 34 91/40 32 79
info@martinluther.de
www.martinluther.de

Castle Church (*Schlosskirche*)
Schlossplatz
Tel.: 0 34 91/40 25 85
Fax: 0 34 91/45 97 26
E-mail: schlosskirche@kirche-wittenberg.de

City Church of St. Mary (*Stadtkirche St. Marien*)
Jüdenstrasse 36
06886 Lutherstadt Wittenberg
Tel.: 0 34 91/62 83-0
Fax: 0 34 91/62 83-11
E-mail: info@kirche-wittenberg.de
www.stadtkirchengemeinde-wittenberg.de
Organ Concerts: A very special musical event in the Castle and
     City Churches
     Castle Church (Ladegast Organ): May–October,
          Tuesdays, 2:30–3 p.m.
     City Church (Sauer Organ): May–October, Fridays, 6 p.m.
     Summer Concerts: May–October in the Castle and City
               Churches, every other Saturday, 5 p.m.

Cranach House (*Cranachhaus*)
Markt 3–4
Cranach Courtyard (*Cranachhof*)
Schlossstrasse 1
Tel.: 0 34 91/4 20 19 11
Fax: 0 34 91/4 20 19 19
E-mail: cranach-stiftung@web.de
     cranach-hoefe@t-online.de
www.cranach-stiftung.de
Business Hours of Cranach House:
April–October: Monday–Saturday, 10 a.m.–5 p.m. and
     Sunday, 1–5 p.m.
November–March: Tuesday–Saturday, 10 a.m.–1 p.m. and
     Sunday, 1–5 p.m.

Bugenhagen House (*Bugenhagenhaus*)
Evangelical City Church Parish in Wittenberg
(*Evangelische Stadtkirchengemeinde Wittenberg*)
Tel.: 0 34 91/62 83-0
Fax: 0 34 91/62 83-11
E-mail: stadtkirche@kirche-wittenberg.de

Chapter 8: Worms

General Information
Worms Tourist Information (*Tourist Information Worms*)
Marktplatz 2
67547 Worms
Tel.: 0 62 41/2 50 45
Fax: 0 62 41/2 63 28
E-mail: touristinfo@worms.de
www.worms.de

Chapter 9: Augsburg

General Information
Augsburg Area Tourism Incorporated
(*Regio Augsburg Tourismus GmbH*)
Schiessgrabenstrasse 14
86150 Augsburg
Tel.: 08 21/50 20 70
E-mail: tourismus@regio-augsburg.de
www.augsburg-tourismus.de

The House on Maximilianstrasse
(*Haus in der Maximilianstrasse*)
Unfortunately, this building where Cardinal Cajetan held Luther's
hearing can be viewed only from the outside.

St. Anne's Church (*St. Anna*)
Fuggerstrasse 8
86150 Augsburg
Tel.: 08 21/34 37 10
Fax: 08 21/34 37-1 24
E-mail: pfarramt@st-anna-augsburg.de
www.st-anna-augsburg.de
Business Hours:
Monday: 12–5 p.m.
Tuesday–Saturday: 10 a.m.–12:30 p.m. and 3–6 p.m. (May 1–
    October 31) **OR** 3–5 p.m. (November 1–April 30)
Sundays/holidays: 10 a.m.–12:30 p.m. (worship services); 3–4 p.m.
The Lutherstiege Museum is next to the church. Its business hours
    are the same as those of the church.

Chapter 10: Torgau

General Information
Torgau Tourism and Resorts Incorporated
(*Torgauer Tourismus & Bäder GmbH*)
Torgau Information Center (*Torgau-Informations-Center*)
Markt 1
04860 Torgau
Tel.: 0 34 21/7 01 40
Fax: 0 34 21/70 14 15
E-mail: info@tic-torgau.de

Hartenfels Castle (*Schloss Hartenfels*)
Schlossstrasse
04860 Torgau
Information is likewise under 0 34 21/70 14-0

The Museum of City and Cultural History
(*Stadt- und Kulturgeschichtliches Museum*)
Includes the room where Katharina von Bora died
    (*Katharina-Luther-Stube*)
Wintergrüne 5
04860 Torgau
E-mail: koenig@museum-torgau.de
www.museum-torgau.de
Business Hours:
Daily, 10 a.m.–6 p.m.

Chapter 11: Eisleben

General Information
Tourist Association of Lutherstadt Eisleben and Mansfeld
(*Fremdenverkehrsverein Lutherstadt Eisleben/Mansfelder
    Land e.V.*)
Bahnhofstrasse 36
06295 Lutherstadt Eisleben
Tel.: 0 34 75/60 21 24 or -1 94 33
Fax: 0 34 75/60 26 34
E-mail: info@eisleben-tourist.de
www.eisleben-tourist.de

Luther's Birth House (*Luthers Geburtshaus*)
Society of Luther Memorials (*Stiftung Luthergedenkstätten*)
Lutherstrasse 15
06295 Lutherstadt Eisleben
Tel.: 0 34 75/71 47 80
Fax: 0 34 75/7 14 78 15

Luther's Death House (*Luthers Sterbehaus*)
Andreaskirchplatz 7
06295 Lutherstadt Eisleben
Tel./Fax: 0 34 75/60 22 85

Church of St. Andrew (*St. Andreas*)
Parish Office:
Petrikirchplatz 22
06295 Lutherstadt Eisleben
Tel.: 0 34 75/60 22 29
Fax: 0 34 75/61 23 45
www.ev-kirche-eisleben-anp.de
Organ Concerts: May 1–September 30, Tuesdays, 12–12:30 p.m.

Church of St. Anne (*St. Annen*)
Annenkirchplatz 2
06295 Lutherstadt Eisleben
Tel.: 0 34 75/60 41 15
Fax: 0 34 75/61 23 45
E-mail: st.annen-eisleben@freenet.de
www.st-annen-eisleben.de
Business Hours:
May–October: Monday–Saturday, 2–4 p.m.
On Sunday, opens after the worship service around 11 a.m.
During the summer months, one worship service each month is
 held with other churches. On these Sundays, the church is
 not open.

Links to Luther and His Works (texts in English)

http://www.cph.org/luthersworks
    (new volumes of Luther in English)
http://www.bookofconcord.org/
http://www.iclnet.org/pub/resources/text/wittenberg/wittenberg-luther.html

Other Books by Martin Luther available from Concordia Publishing House (1-800-325-3040 • www.cph.org)
- Luther's Works: American Edition, vols. 1–54
- Luther's Works on CD-ROM
- *What Luther Says*, edited by Ewald Plass

Timeline

1463   Birth of Frederick the Wise, Saxon prince from 1486 to 1525

1472   Birth of Lucas Cranach

1483   November 10: Birth of Martin Luther in Eisleben; November 11: Luther's Baptism

1484   Luther family moves to Mansfeld

1488   Luther attends the Latin school

1497   Luther attends school with the Brethren of the Common Life in Magdeburg

1498   Luther moves to Eisenach; attends the parish school of St. George

1501   May: Luther enrolls at the University of Erfurt

1505   January: Luther is awarded a Master of Arts degree; May: begins law school; July 2: Thunderstorm experience at Stotternheim; July 17: Luther enters the Augustinian Monastery in Erfurt

1507   April 3: Luther's ordination; begins theological studies

1508   Lucas Cranach receives his hereditary emblem, a winged snake, from Electoral Prince Frederick the Wise

1510   November: Luther travels to Rome

1511   Luther returns from Rome; transfers to Wittenberg

1512   October 19: Luther is awarded his Doctor of Theology degree

1513   Luther's "Tower Experience" (*Turmerlebnis*)

1517   October 31: Luther posts his Ninety-five Theses against indulgences

1518   "Sermon on Indulgence and Grace"; August 7: Luther is summoned to Rome, to no avail; October 12–14: Hearing with Cardinal Cajetan, at which Luther refuses to recant

1519   Death of Emperor Maximilian; election of Charles V as emperor; July 4–14: disputation between Luther and Eck

1520   Legal proceedings against Luther are taken up again; the papal bull *Exsurge Domine* threatens excommunication; August: "Address to the Christian Nobility of the German Nation"; December: public burning of the bull threatening excommunication

1521   January 3: Imposition of excommunication on Luther by the bull *Decet Romanum Pontificem*; March: Luther is summoned before the Imperial Diet of Worms; April 17 / 18: Luther's appearance before the Imperial Diet of Worms; April 26: Luther departs from Worms; May 4: Luther arrives at the Wartburg; May 8: Luther is declared an outlaw by the Edict of Worms; December: Luther begins his translation of the New Testament.

1522   January 6: The Augustinian congregation in Wittenberg is disbanded; March 1–6: Luther returns to Wittenberg because of the unrest and the iconoclasm there; April: Zwingli begins the Reformation in Zurich; September: publication of Luther's translation of the New Testament

1523   March: Luther writes "On Temporal Authority"; July 1: the first martyrs are burned in Brussels; Luther writes his first hymns

1524   June: The beginning of the Peasants' War in the Black Forest; October: Luther stops wearing his monastic robes

1525   Peasants' War; Luther writes *Against the Heavenly Prophets*; Luther travels to Saxony and Thuringia, gives sermons against the revolts; June 13: Luther marries Katharina von Bora; December: Luther writes *The Bondage of the Will*, a reply to *The Freedom of the Will* by Erasmus

1526   The Imperial Diet of Speyer postpones the enforcement of the Edict of Worms according to the (temporary) ruling "whose the region, his the religion" (*cuius regio, eius religio*)

1529   October: Marburg Colloquy with Zwingli

Bibliography

The abbreviations used in the endnotes are in parentheses.

Bainton, Roland H. *Martin Luther*. Translated by Hermann Dörries. 3d ed. Göttingen, 1959. Title of the original English edition: *Here I Stand: A Life of Martin Luther*.

Brecht, Martin. *Martin Luther*. 3 vols. Stuttgart, 1986 (Brecht).

Bretschneider, Carolus Gottlieb, ed. *Corpus Reformatorum* (CR). Vol. 11. Halle, 1843.

Beutel, Albrecht. *Luther Handbuch*. Tübingen, 2005.

Hürlimann, Martin, ed. *Martin Luther dargestellt von seinen Freunden und Zeitgenossen etc.* Berlin, 1933 (Hürlimann).

Junghans, Helmer. *Martin Luther und Wittenberg*. Munich, 1996.

Köstlin, Julius. *Martin Luther: Sein Leben und seine Schriften*. Vols. 1–2. 2d ed. Eberfeld, 1883 (Köstlin).

Lilje, Hans. *Luther*. Reinbeck bei Hamburg, 1965. 17th ed., 1994.

Luther, Martin. *D. Martin Luthers Werke: Kritische Gesamtausgabe* (WA). 73 vols. in 85. Weimar: H. Böhlau, 1883–.

———. *D. Martin Luthers Werke: Briefwechsel* (WA Br). 18 vols. Weimar: H. Böhlau, 1930–.

———. *D. Martin Luthers Werke: Deutsche Bibel* (WA DB). 12 vols. in 15. Weimar: H. Böhlau, 1906–.

———. *D. Martin Luthers Werke: Tischreden* (WA TR). 6 vols. Weimar: H. Böhlau, 1912–21.

———. *Dr. Martin Luthers sämmtliche Schriften: Neue revidirte Stereotypausgabe* (StL). 23 vols. in 25. St. Louis: Concordia, 1880–1910.

———. *Die gantze Heilige Schrifft Deudsch 1545*. Edited by Hans Volz and Heinz Blanke. Reprinted in 2 vols. (Volz).

Matthesius, M. Johann. *D. Martin Luthers Leben in siebzehn Predigten*. Edited by Georg Buchwald. Leipzig, 1887 (Matthesius).

Mechthild von Magdeburg. *Das fließende Licht der Gottheit: Eine Auswahl*. Edited by Gisela Vollmann-Profe. Stuttgart: Reclam, 2008.

Oberman, Heiko. *Luther, Mensch zwischen Gott und Teufel*. Berlin, 1982.

Schlisske, Otto. *Handbuch der Lutherlieder*. Göttingen, 1948 (Schlisske).

Steinwachs, Albrecht, and Jürgen Pietsch. *Die Stadtkirche der Lutherstadt Wittenberg*. Wittenberg, 2000.

Treu, Martin. *Luther und Torgau*. Wittenberg, 1995.

———. *Katharina von Bora*. Wittenberg, 1995.

Warnke, Martin. *Cranachs Luther*. Frankfurt am Main, 1984.

Acknowledgments, Image Credits, and Permissions

© 2008 Dr. Cornelia Dömer: p. 2 (Luther's birth house); p. 12 (Wartburg close-up); p. 86 (Wartburg: Luther's workroom from the outside); p. 14 (Luther House in Eisenach); p. 26 (entry of the Augustinian monastery in Erfurt); p. 30 (garden of the Augustinian monastery in Erfurt); p. 35 (Luther House in Wittenberg, formerly a cloister); pp. 38, 52 (Luther Monument, Market Square in Wittenberg); p. 39 (city hall); U1-Klappe, p. 50 (Melanchthon House); p. 51 (Market Square and city church of St. Mary's); p. 52 (broad side of city hall); p. 53 (Cranach Courtyard at a high angle); p. 68 (bust of Johannes Bugenhagen); p. 97 (Torgau Articles; information sign about the old superintendency); p. 100 (Castle Torgau [Hartenfels Castle], gate arch); p. 100 (Castle Torgau [Hartenfels Castle], inner courtyard); p. 100 (Torgau, Castle Church portal); p. 100 (Torgau, Castle Church portal detail); p. 101 (city church of St. Mary's; grave plate of Katharina von Bora [entire]); p. 101 (city church of St. Mary's); p. 106 (065_Wittenberg Luthergrab Platte_CD_101-0115_ IMG.JPG); p. 109 (Luther Monument in Eisleben); p. 109 (Luther's death house).

shutterstock.com: p. 16 (Wartburg at evening), © Joerg Humpe; p. 17 (Wartburg cannons), © Ulrich Willmünder; p. 20 (cathedral, narrow side), © Andrea Seemann; p. 21 (Erfurt roofs), © guentermanaus; p. 22 (Erfurt Church of the Barefooted Monks), © Andrea Seemann; p. 23 (Erfurt cathedral entrance), © Andrea Seemann; p. 27 (Erfurt cathedral), © Andrea Seemann; p. 33 (Basilica of St. Peter [Vatican]), © Margita; p. 80 (city wall), © Oxana Zubov; p. 85 (Wartburg at night), © Joerg Humpe; p. 90 (Augsburg Town Hall Square; *Perlachturm* dating to Luther's time), © Bob Cheung; p. 94 (old barrel), © Andrew McDonough; p. 94 (grain), © Semjonow Juri; p. 127 (information symbol), © Bruno B.; p. 136 (open Luther Bible), © Hannah Gleghorn.

Endnotes

1 WA TR 5, no. 5362 n. 4; cf. Brecht 1:14, 6 n. 5.

2 WA TR 5, no. 6250 (after 1530), *cum ille dixisset, me fore* = "whereas that one said, I should . . ."

3 Cf. http://www.mansfeld-lutherstadt.de

4 According to http://www.heiligenlexikon.de/BiographienA/Anna.htm

5 See pp. 18–19.

6 Mechthild von Magdeburg, *Das fliessende Licht der Gottheit* 5:34.

7 http://www.heiligenlexikon.de/BiographienE/Elisabeth_von_Thueringen.htm

8 WA TR 3, no. 2871b, line 20.

9 The room where a chapter of the Bible was read aloud each day.

10 Cf. http://www.erfurt-web.de The sum of the Latin letters' numerical value reveals the year of the building's completion.

11 Brecht 1:57.

12 Brecht 1:461; the following wealth of sources are cited: WA 8:573.20ff.; WA TR 1, no. 116; WA TR 4, nos. 4414 and 4407; WA TR 5, no. 5373; WA Br 384, 80.

13 WA TR 5, no. 6250.

14 Brecht 1:60.

15 This prayer reads as follows in the English language: "Hail, Queen, Mother of mercy, our life, our delight, and our hope, hail! To you we call out as banished children of Eve. To you we sigh, mourning and weeping in this vale of tears. So then, O advocate of ours, turn your merciful eyes toward us and after this misery, show us Jesus, the blessed fruit of your womb, O kind, gentle, sweet Virgin Mary."

16 Special ordinances.

17 The title for a leader of a monastic order.

18 Brecht 1:105.

19 The income required for spiritual service.

20 Namely, in the Gospel (Romans 1:17).

21 The translation of the last sentence is based on Brecht 1:219.

22 Romans 1:17.

23 Through faith the gift of justification is thus received.

24 WA 54:185f.

25 WA Br 5:445.2ff.

26 See also Irene Dingel, "Luther und Wittenberg," in *Luther Handbuch*, ed. Albrecht Beutel (Tübingen, 2005).

27 See also Junghans, *Luther und Wittenberg.*

28 The routes of these streams have been reopened during the current city's renovation.

29 That is, six additional clergymen lived on it.

30 The remains of deceased saints. Meditation on these relics that was subject to fees granted an indulgence, that is, remission of guilt and punishment (see below).

31 See also Junghans, *Luther und Wittenberg.*

32 For details about her, see below.

33 WA Br 11:148–49, no. 4139. See also Köstlin 2:618f.

34 Köstlin 2:619.

35 Based on StL 1:271f.

36 Naming himself "Karlstadt" after his hometown, see below.

37 See also the section "Luther and the Jews" (pp. 113–15).

38 The rabbi who offers the nourishment is not depicted as a pig but as a man, though he turns others into suckling piglets through harmful nourishment.

39 "Jehovah," actually "Yahweh," translated without exception by the apostles in the New Testament as "Lord."

40 That is referring to the swastika of the National Socialists.

41 http://de.wikipedia.org/wiki/
Rathaus_%28Lutherstadt_Wittenberg%29

42 Cf. http://www.baufachinformation.de/denkmalpflege.
jsp?md=2001017177233

43 Cf. http://www.cranach-stiftung.de

44 WA TR 1, no. 49.

45 See also Treu, *Luther und Torgau.*

46 Thus his well-known formula in the Small Catechism. However, he did reject the notion of equal rights; see his commentary on Ephesians 5:22; Colossians 3:18; and 1 Peter 3:2:

"First, it is [God's] will that wives should be subject to their husbands" (StL 3:1233.18).

47 Martin Luther, "To the Councilmen of All Cities in Germany, That They Establish and Maintain Christian Schools (1524)," WA 15:33.5.

48 WA Br 9:505.12; in German: StL 21b:2641.

49 WA Br 10:176.14; in German: StL 21b:2800.

50 WA Br 10:520.32; in German: StL 21b:2950f.

51 See also Dingel, "Luther und Wittenberg," 168–79.

52 WA TR 5, no. 5375c (1540).

53 See also Christian Peters, "Luther and Melanchthon," in *Luther Handbuch*, ed. Albrecht Beutel (Tübingen, 2005).

54 Brecht 2:60.

55 See also Steinwachs and Pietsch, *Die Stadtkirche der Lutherstadt Wittenberg*.

56 WA 51:531.13ff.

57 To save space, only a selection of Luther's Theses is printed here. All ninety-five are available on the Internet, for example, under http://www.iclnet.org/pub/resources/text/wittenberg/luther/web/ninetyfive.html

58 Brecht 1:194.

59 Brecht 1:200.

60 Brecht 1:198.

61 In Latin: WA Br 1:325.12ff.

62 Roman Catholic ecclesiastical laws.

63 In Latin: WA Br 2:234.4ff.; in German: StL 21a:324, no. 356.

64 www.bautz.de

65 In Latin: WA Br 2:380.56ff.; in German: StL 15:2524f.

66 For the original version and orthography, see Volz 2:1962.19ff.

67 StL 14:91 n. 3.

68 Matthew 12:34.

69 WA TR 2:639.28ff.

70 Luther had enclosed the hymns "From Depths of Woe I Cry to You" and "May God Bestow on Us His Grace."

71 WA Br 3:220.1ff.

72 Schlisske, 116.

73 Cf. Martin Rössler, *Liedermacher im Gesangbuch: Liedgeschichte in Lebensbildern* (Stuttgart, 2001), 35–81.

74 WA Br 8:51.5–15.

75 Brecht 3:229.

76 StL 2:553.63.

77 Brecht 3:229.

78 See below his remarks about the plague.

79 It is regarded as the first new Lutheran church building.

80 WA Br 11:269.3; for a somewhat variant form: StL 21b:3186.3.

81 Cf. http://www.torgau.eu/p/d2.asp?artikel_id=1067

82 Matthesius, 360f.

83 CR 11:730.3.

84 WA 53:587.1ff.

85 Such as "On the Ineffable Name and the Lineage of Christ," WA 53:573–648.

86 Concerning the German word used, see WA 53:600 n. 5.

87 WA 53:600.26ff.

88 WA 53:412ff.

89 WA 53:526.12.

90 Brecht 3:345.

91 StL 16:173.67.

92 StL 16:121.2 and 4.

93 StL 16:172.60–61.

94 StL 16:173.68.

95 In Latin: WA 7:94ff. and especially 142.23ff.; in German: WA 7.

96 In German: StL 8:1600.

97 WA 18:600.15ff.

98 WA 18:786.30ff.

99 WA 18:783.17ff., 783.28ff.

100 See also Oberman, *Luther*.

101 Erasmus of Rotterdam, cited in: P. S. and H. M. Allen, ed., *Opus Epistolarum Des. Erasmi Roterodami*, vol. 5: *1522–1524* (Oxford, 1924), 327.3ff., no. 1384.